Journey with My Selves

DOROTHY LIVESAY

Journey with My Selves

A MEMOIR
1909-1963

Douglas & McIntyre
Vancouver/Toronto

Douglas & McIntyre Ltd.
1615 Venables Street
Vancouver, British Columbia V5L 2H1

Canadian Cataloguing in Publication Data
Livesay, Dorothy.
Journey with my selves
ISBN 0-88894-714-3
1. Livesay, Dorothy, 1909- —Biography. 2. Poets, Canadian (English)—20th century—Biography.*
I. Title.
PS8523.I82Z53 1991   C811'.54   C91-091160-6
PR9199.3.L58Z469 1991

Portions of this book have appeared, in slightly different form, in the following publications: "Winnipeg Days" is adapted from *Beginnings* (Peguis Publishers, 1988); "Gina" appeared in *Event* and in the *Contemporary Authors Autobiography Series*, Volume 8 (Gale, 1989); "On Being in Love" appeared in *NeWest*; "Strange Encounter: Raymond Knister" appeared in *Books in Canada*, and "Moving West" was originally published in *This Magazine*.
The lines from "Spain" are reprinted by permission of Faber and Faber Ltd. from *Selected Poems* by W. H. Auden.
The manuscript was edited by Marc Côté with the assistance of a Canada Council Explorations Grant.

Substantive and copy editing for the press by Barbara Pulling
Design: Robert MacDonald / MediaClones
Cover photograph of the author, taken in 1936, and other photographs courtesy Department of Archives and Special Collections, The University of Manitoba

Printed and bound in Canada by D. W. Friesen & Sons Ltd.
Printed on acid-free paper ∞

For Anne Rosman Campbell,
over fifty years my confidante,
supporter and critic

Contents

Preface / 9

Introduction / 11
Winnipeg Days / 17
Moving to Toronto / 25
Parents: An Unarranged Marriage / 32
Belief and Unbelief / 54
Gina / 59
The Writing Game / 88
Rites of Passage / 101
On Being in Love / 119
Strange Encounter: Raymond Knister / 129
Consequences / 138
Crossing the Border / 144
Moving West / 152
The Guide: Virgil / 159
Malcolm and Me / 167
Family Lives / 172
La Vita Nuova / 198
After Words / 219

Books by Dorothy Livesay / 221

Preface

It is well that a memoir spanning a lifetime will have emerged from several versions chosen by the author: some to be renovated, altered and rejected, some enlightened by the perspicacity of editorial critics and concerned friends. I am indeed grateful for "The Dorothy Livesay Issue" of *Room of One's Own*, edited by Jean Wilson, and for the perceptions of Anne Foster, Jane Haig and Sandra Hutchinson. In particular I appreciate having Lon Lawson's permission to quote from the letters of his wife, Jean Watts Lawson, and for permission from long-time friend and critic Leon Edel to publish his views on Raymond Knister's death. My special thanks go to my secretarial helpers for their patience and enthusiasm over the years.

In the long run I am the editor of this book, ready to accept praise or blame, in the hope that it will give readers a taste of the variety and spice to be found in the growth of our Canadian culture.

Introduction

Sometimes one's life, looked back upon, appears to be enclosed in a series of Chinese boxes. Each one taken by itself seems to have no significance; but when fitted, each within the next size, a pattern is visualized, there is a sense of completion. So it has been with my desire to live fully, overflowing into friendships of all kinds, and at the same time to put it down. Out of experience to create something new.

Recently I visited Erindale College and nearby St. Peter's Cemetery where my parents are buried. They never knew that the villages of Erindale and Clarkson would be melded into Mississauga, a suburb of Toronto. And Marine Drive had become a wandering paved road with new houses on every lot. I passed the spot where Mazo de la Roche had her studio cottage and had left her mark on a street sign: Jalna. Next to this, at 1219, I stopped and saw that my father's house, Woodlot, was still standing.

The house had not changed much from how I remembered it. All the original characteristics were in good repair. The clapboard was painted brown as it had been, though maybe a little darker, and the Georgian door with fan window above and glass panels either side was still trimmed with white. On the grounds I could see blooming the rare red trilliums, their common cousins the white, then the small violets, the bloodroot and the hepaticas, all of which my father had transplanted from the woods in Erindale. Forty, fifty years ago, my sister, Sophie, and I had helped my father do this by carrying slabs of shale from the cold creek to his parked car and then from his car to

Woodlot, Clarkson, Ontario, 1941

deposit them where he indicated so they could be used as the basis for his rose garden. Beyond were the trees that Sophie and I, former prairie children aged nine and eleven, had discovered and plunged into in the month of May, with its breathtaking cherry and apple blossoms. For us, then, the trees came to be almost as real as people; the maple, oak and cedar were as distant friends, but the slim silver birches were embraceable. On moonlit nights I used to walk closer to them and place my cheek against the bark to listen to the pulsing sap. It was after such nights of listening to the birches, now frail and tottering, and to the flutelike song of the whippoorwill that as a young girl I was ready to imagine stories and find the words for poems.

Perhaps because his father and a brother were architects, my father felt he had a natural bent for this art and so designed Woodlot himself. It was built on land bought from his distant relatives, the Harrises, in what was then called Clarkson. The Georgian door which he designed to be an exact copy of the ones in Dublin served as the main entrance. Inside, he laid down a shining oak floor, which reflected the fireplace with its three centre stones, collected one from the Pacific coast, one from the Atlantic and one from the great shield in Ontario. There were Italian lamps, ordered from Europe, hanging from cedar beams salvaged from the home of other relatives. To this were added Oriental rugs, Chinese ceramic horses and the Jacobean hope chest, an heirloom from my father's mother's family, the Blighs.

The present owners of the house welcomed me in. It was a real pleasure to see how little had changed. My father's possessions had of course been removed, but the house itself had undergone few alterations. Now there was wall-to-wall carpeting, which hid the oak floor, and the kitchen had been modernized.

This house, Woodlot, is where I had spent my weekends, away from Glen Mawr School and, later, Trinity College. Here I escaped from study to have free time to write or read at will. I had no household chores to do, no dishes to wash or beds to make, as there was always a housekeeper in charge. While I wrote or read, my father disappeared to his log cabin in the woods, away from the telephone and "the wimmin"; my mother sat in the sunroom writing poems or translating Ukrainian folk songs or working on a piece of freelance journalism, and my sister went sketching, taking the dog with her. Next door, in summer, Mazo de la Roche was writing the Jalna novels. It seemed to be an ideal country life, but the prim Ontario farming community looked rather askance at us, regarding us as "the mad Livesays."

All these memories came back to me as I stood by the bay window, looking out to where there was now a pond with two aggressive white geese guarding it where once there had been a stream with masses of daffodils and irises along its banks. So much time had passed and, yet, so little had been altered inside the doors of my father's house.

In writing memoirs, conflict arises when one seems obliged to choose between using recorded material from the past – diaries, letters, essays and stories – or relying upon memories. Malcolm Muggeridge believed that memoir evokes those important impressions, emotions and events that have truly influenced our lives. Whereas the daily journal, so significant when first written, would, he felt, be irrelevant years later.

The next perplexing question is Pilate's "What is truth?" My father, John Frederick Bligh Livesay (JFB), was faced with this question when in his sixties he began to work on his autobiography. "The truth, the truth!" he told me. "If only I could write the truth." The scraps of his writing still extant show how he sought to speak of events and men, the beginnings and growth of the Canadian Press, as clearly as he, with his inside view as general manager for twenty years, saw them. "But Live! You can't say that," my mother, Florence Randal Livesay (FRL), would tell him. "That would be libel." All his journalistic life my father had dealt with the working problems of libel. Yet how could the truth be libellous? He turned to Montaigne and in his favourite essayist he sought the answer. Perhaps he found it, and died. There, beside his bed, were Montaigne's essays, open on the little square table with the ivory paper cutter between the pages. I like to think the words were:

We have lived enough for others; let us live at least this remaining bit of life for ourselves. Let us bring back our thoughts and plans to ourselves and our comfort...let us break free from these violent clutches that engage us elsewhere and draw us away from ourselves. That is to say, let the other things be ours, but not joined and glued to us so strongly that they cannot be detached without tearing off our skin. The greatest thing in the world is to know how to belong to ourselves.

Be that as it may, the truth my father was seeking could, in the end, only be relative. His view of men and women and events was deeply coloured by his own personality and beliefs. What he handed on to me was the imprint of himself, not the imprint of facts.

"What is truth?" I like Emily Dickinson's evasive answer: "Tell all the Truth but tell it slant." Autobiography, or memoirs, are not written to satisfy a secret personal urge. They are written by an actor who performs behind a mask. The aim must be to attract an audience. A formidable task; and one much akin to that of the novelist.

My perspective on events and people is undoubtedly lopsided, slanted, with many unavoidable gaps, tempered by my own early view of my parents, brought up as I was with so many inhibitions implanted by my mother and so many ideas of freedom urged by my father. It is small wonder I have found it hard to disclose my inner life to the public. But I am the sum of all these perspectives; what I hope to present, therefore, throughout these pages, is a series of selves, views of myself. I am not ashamed to set down what seems to be the truth of my parents' lives nor what seems to be the truth of the lives of the men and women who have informed my consciousness since leaving the parental fold. These people who have demanded my love and attention have also become a part of me, and to set them down in these pages is not to relinquish them, but to remember. Always with longing, to remember. This is my truth.

*A young D.L. in her "bunny suit," a present sent from England by her
grandmother Sophy Bligh Livesay*

Winnipeg Days

I was born in Winnipeg on October 12, 1909, during the first snowstorm of the year. After my sister, Sophie, arrived three years later, we moved to Lipton Street, where we lived in a small two-storey white clapboard house in a lower middle-class neighbourhood. The wooden sidewalks had been down long enough to require new boards sometimes, fresh-scented golden boards from the sawmill. Grass grew with difficulty on the narrow boulevard between the sidewalk and the paved road, and timid, spindly young elms had been planted at intervals, just near enough to the curb for the Eaton's horse to reach, stretching his neck to nibble the tender leaves. On this unprepossessing street my father had chosen a corner lot, which gave him some scope for his passion for fence building. Kitty-corner across the street was the west-end firehall, which housed those great grey stallions, ever ready, when the huge red doors sprung open, to do their daily rehearsal. In summertime I would sit safely on our front porch steps surrounded by flower beds. Inside this domain there were dazzling arrangements of poppy, bachelor's-button, sweet william; masses of portulaca and nasturtium, purple pools of pansy and the whole of this punctuated by the scent of mignonette. All old-fashioned English flowers were these, a reminder of my father's Isle of Wight origin, still considered home. But in these flowers, these reminders, my father took a quiet pride, as he lay resting on the screened-in porch at one side of the house, listening to the complimentary exclamations of passers-by.

Father's flowers, however, left my sister and me with almost nowhere to play. The grass plot in the centre was hardly big enough for a doll buggy or a pretend house made of chairs and blankets. We learned soon enough to avoid at all costs touching any of Father's projects. If we wanted to run or play tag, it had to be in the back kitchen garden, where he had made a large circular bed of rich black Manitoba loam. Here, strong and flavourful, grew green peas, scarlet runner beans, carrots and corn, flanked at the back end of the oval with a trellis of Mother's favourite flower, the sweet pea. Father had made a circular path around the vegetable garden, using the winter's ashes as a base. This was quite good for running on. But outside of this cinder path and circling the high wooden fence, there were more and more flowers: the tall spiky ones like hollyhock, larkspur and delphinium in every shade of blue. Only in one cool corner, next to the back porch, did we have any play space. Father made us a sandpile there, and later a slide built of heavy planks; a wide winter slide this, onto which pails of water were poured, only to freeze instantly into a glassy mirror. On frosty days, seated on tin trays, we were the envy of the neighbourhood, as we banged our way up and down this homemade rollercoaster.

The differences between boys and girls began in early childhood, in the games we played. During the long Winnipeg winters, we girls went sliding and sled-pulling together. The boys threw snowballs, built forts or used the street for hockey practice. We built snowmen and used lumps of coal for the eyes, a carrot for the nose and Father's pipe for the mouth. We also made angels, tossing ourselves backward into freshly fallen snow, arms outspread. All this time the boys either ignored us or scorned our efforts.

For summer days, out came the skipping ropes, brightly coloured ropes with red handles. Or, after much coaxing of parents, a long and heavy ship's rope that was shared by several little girls for practising jumping and for marathon skippings of double Dutch. Once, a boy passed by, sneering but interested. We told him if he wanted to join us, we were willing to show him how. His answer was that he would bet he didn't need to learn, he was sure he could skip, "first try." Reluctantly, we handed him a rope and, after a few stumbles, of course he could do it. His response to this was to drop the rope and let us know that skipping was easy, that girls' games were all easy.

Another girls' game was jacks. Two of us would play, sitting on the verandah steps, taking turns at bouncing the small, hard rubber ball and picking up one jack, then two, then three, then four. I wonder if I could play this game now, with all the dexterity it requires.

Birthday parties were the events that made me overly nervous. I had to put on my best white or pink dress, which always had frills, and white stockings and black patent leather slippers. In one hand I clutched the birthday present wrapped in white tissue paper tied with blue ribbon. With the hot sun blazing down on me, I would walk the two or three blocks on the wooden sidewalk. Heart beating, I'd press the bell. Inside, I was asked to come and join the games of Pin the Tail on the Donkey and Blind Man's Bluff. And along would come the moment, almost inevitably, of being a loser, of having to kneel down, blindfolded, to the sound of, "Heavy, heavy hangs over your head, what shall your forfeit be?" Once, when named to kiss a boy, who touched my arm and said: "Come on, let's do it," I ran away into a bedroom and closed the door behind me. This was not being a good sport, yet no amount of jeering or begging could bring me out of the room. Only the call for ice cream and birthday cake could lure me, to sit far away from the boy who wanted to "do it."

There is another event from those early years that I have never been able to forget. Some boys were playing on our street and in a tree in our yard they discovered a robin's nest. One of the boys climbed up into the tree and threw all the eggs down to the ground. The robins screamed in agony. I stood looking at this, but was unable to do anything. I hated those boys for what they were doing; I hated them.

Chores and jobs were always different for girls and boys. Girls watered the flower garden, boys mowed the lawn. The energetic boys were encouraged to push their fathers' lawn mowers from door to door, offering to cut the neighbour lady's lawn for twenty-five cents. Girls were permitted, on the same basis, to baby-sit. We never dreamed of delivering papers, as that was a whole world unto itself, a world of rivalry and commerce that the boys were learning, and, it seemed, were supposed to learn.

When I was six, the woman across the street, Mrs. Betts, wanted to pay me for looking after her little boy. At first my mother refused to allow me to accept money for this. Mrs. Betts insisted, however, that I be paid for my efforts. Finally, my mother suggested I make a little bank, pasted together like a basket out of green office paper, and here I could save the money given me until I had enough to send to the Belgian children. By this time I knew, from reading the headlines, that there were children in the world who did not have warm clothing for winter, nor good meals every day. I was taught that I had to "give up" for them. As my horizons expanded more and more, beyond home and neighbourhood, I became aware of a world quite different from the child's reality of games and "pretend."

At a very early age I saw my words in print. My mother, who wrote a column for the *Winnipeg Free Press*, occasionally quoted "Dorothy's Sayings." These ranged from the word plays I made, saying *wintersaults* instead of *somersaults*, to short conversations with my mother:

"I think angels should come and take the children."

"But why, dear?"

"Because God would look after the children much better than their mothers do!"

One wonders if at three I felt myself to be a neglected child. I don't remember feeling this way. Later, at five or six probably, I felt that my mother was sharing her work with me, getting me interested in what she was writing on the typewriter. When schoolchildren, especially those from Indian reserves and residential schools, began writing letters to her as a columnist, my mother urged them to write their stories, just as she had urged me to tell her some. These stories, too, were published, and when printed were cut out and kept in a scrapbook. I

D.L. (front) and her sister, Sophie, 1916

suppose she showed me the printed words long before I could read
them, but an impression was made on me and I became conscious of
what my imagination envisioned. Nonetheless, I saw my parents busy
at writing every day, and I was sometimes taken down by street car to
the Free Press building where my father's office, the Western Associated Press, was installed. The pressroom, thundering away with
typewriters and reporters wearing green eyeshades, gave me a feeling
of identification with the outside world of adults. Especially when the
ruddy-headed, gruff editor, John Dafoe, would pass by and pat me on
the head.

It must be the same for children who grow up in a musical family,
or who have parents with as strong an interest and involvement in
sports. My education in writing owes much to my parents; writing was
their world and it became mine.

I do not remember the beginning of World War I, but my emotions
were early affected by the feverish excitement. Perhaps that was the last
time in our century when people approached war as a glamourous
event. At any rate, I remember playing in the front yard and suddenly
hearing the beat of drums and the skirl of pipes. Around the corner
came the Black Watch, playing the bagpipes, their kilts whirling. Like
every child on the street I tore along beside them, skipping and
jumping with excitement.

The serious side of war, however, was soon to impinge. The
newspaper played a key part: at first it was the "Extra" that excited me,
news of victories shouted by newspaper boys down a dark night street.
In daylight I used to imitate the boys, bundling together a pile of old
newspapers and marching about, shouting my own version of "Extra,
extra!" But soon that call was regarded with fear and anxiety, for
regardless of the news, good or bad, there would be casualty lists. Every
day my mother went over the casualty lists, commenting on the young
men she knew, or telephoning my grandmother to discuss who was
"missing."

Soon, my uncle Arthur Randal, my mother's brother, went off to war. My father made further attempts every month to get there himself, but there were cogent obstacles in his way: he had weak eyesight, he had a wife and two children, and, most importantly, he had a "key" job working for the Western Associated Press, which was serving all the newspapers of the west with a wire service from overseas.

There was a great hunger for news, with the pervading feeling that the outside world was important. Though still young, I did not escape from this feeling. Long winter nights when I could not sleep I would call out to my mother that I was "too stretchy." That best described the odd sensations and pains in my legs. To soothe me, my mother would play Beethoven sonatas on the piano downstairs, while upstairs my father relieved the ache in the muscles of my legs by massaging them gently. I was recovering, I believe, from rheumatic fever.

There were nights at the beginning of the war years when my father's cousins, the Blighs, would come over for an evening of singing. The Bligh sisters and their brother Bertie were all fine singers. Bessie, who was generously built, full bosomed, had a particularly good contralto voice and she might have been, in other circumstances, an opera singer. But this would have been demeaning; after all, her father had married an East Indian princess. So Bessie worked in a bank and Bertie, her dark and equally talented brother, gave up singing and went off to the war. Within a week he died in the trenches, and his death shattered my mother, I think, far more than it did my father. As a small child who had loved to hear Bertie sing, I too felt the loss keenly. His death left me with a sense of confusion about the adult world, and with a fear of loss.

Some time later, I stayed over at my grandmother's house. She came in at night to hear me say my prayers. I knelt by the bed and, to close the prayer, finished with, "And God bless Mummy and Daddy and Sister and kill all the bad Germans and help us win the war!" My grandmother was appalled to hear this and quickly asked who had taught me to say such a prayer. My answer was clear: "I just say it." I had merely found words to express the feeling I sensed in the air. Next, I was asked if my mother had heard me saying the prayer. I answered that she told me to say it. But I was confused. "Don't you want it, Granny? Don't you want the war to end and Uncle to come home?" The war ending and the killing of the "bad" Germans were one and the same thought to me. My grandmother replied that of course she wanted the war to end, but she then gave me a new idea to think about, one I hadn't heard about or sensed. What if there were a little girl just like me, who wanted her uncle to come home, but she was *German*? I was then tucked in and told, perhaps ironically, not to worry over this.

Children are said to be resilient, adaptable, but this is not so. The only reason they move so easily is because, like puppies, they are lifted up bodily by the scruff of the neck and set down in a new environment. Of their own free will, they would never choose to move. For a child's life is essentially static. One place, one time, is happiness; simply to be held; and there is no movement except within that frame.

Contrariwise, an adult is always conscious of a goal. He or she must be going somewhere, and sometimes this involves a long jump, a new place. The children, of course, are simply expected to adjust to the new pattern, without protest and with very little explanation. So it was, at long last, in 1918, that my father finally attained his heart's desire: he had been accepted as a war correspondent. By listening hard to grown-up conversations (without seeming to), one thing was clear to me: Father wasn't going to shoot with a gun; he would be safe enough; he was only going to write, not to fight.

Moving to Toronto

What are little girls made of, made of
What are little girls made of?
Sugar and spice and all things nice
That's what little girls are made of.

Kind aunts and uncles sang that song to me as a child and made me feel "all smiley." Yet I knew it couldn't be true. It was a story and stories were made up. That was why when you were telling a story you were also telling a lie. Then there was the other side of the nursery rhyme world: the little girl who "when she was good she was very very good / And when she was bad she was horrid." As a child I was trained rigorously to distinguish between good and bad, right and wrong. In adolescence the adult standards I'd adopted began to be questioned and then to crumble. Was there really a right and a wrong?

Nonetheless, the desire to make a story of one's life is one of our most human characteristics. Memory plays us false, yet it reveals more than statistics do. The truth is a many-sided prism and all one person can do is to flash the daylight on some of the walls she knows best.

When we came from Winnipeg to Toronto in 1921, I was a naive twelve-year-old, alternately spoiled and neglected, living in my own imaginative retreat. Because I was supposed to be high-strung, I had had little formal education. But the time before puberty is the time for romping, and before we really got settled in a house in Toronto's Annex district, I had a whiff of experience that would probably have been commonplace among public-school children.

Out of a few such incidents, I remember one that occurred in a boarding house where our family of four first stayed while waiting to find a house to rent. I had to sleep on a cot in the dining room, blinds drawn. One evening, just after I had got into bed, the younger son of the house came in from the kitchen and began to tickle me and then to wrestle. I probably laughed too loud, because the sliding doors that led to the parlour opened and the landlady found us. "Gordon!" she cried. "Out you go, this instant!" As for me, I was just a young puppy flexing my muscles. Later, I told my mother, "We were only playing." But I overheard the two women speaking with concern about Gordon's obsession with girls. "And he's only twelve! His brother never did anything like that." It was Gordon's tall, lean, seventeen-year-old brother on whom I really had the crush.

Those streets of the Annex still exist, although many blocks of houses have been demolished by the growth of the University of Toronto. Willcocks Street, where painter and scholar Barker Fairley lived, has the same red brick semidetached houses, small and discreet with pocket handkerchief lawns. But where are the overhanging elms that I remember being astonished by, so much taller they were than Winnipeg trees? In the Toronto Annex there were always two places to play: the backyard with its high wooden fence, apple, plum or pear tree, green patch of lawn and rhubarb plot; or the street, not yet overtaken by automobiles and so still the territory of schoolchildren.

In those days boys and girls did not mix or meet in twos. On Albany Avenue, where we spent part of our first year, I stole glances across the street at the doctor's son, Evan Withrow; on Walmer Road, I watched John Pennyfather and his brother playing catch, and I watched them watching me. They were different because they were Catholics. Even though I was a friend to their younger sister, we would never mingle. So the valentine I received that February when I was home with the mumps was not a love letter from a boy. I dreamed that it was, but I knew it wasn't. I was just a tomboy without any skills of attraction: plump, freckled, wearing glasses, able to hold my own only with the younger boys and, in summer, go fishing off the dock at Sparrow Lake.

At 77 Walmer Road I sought compensation by creating dramatic games for the younger children on the street. After school, half a dozen would come over to our place to play a complicated fairy-tale routine called Old Witch. In the winter I created a five-pin show in which the neighbouring children did a dance and a play under my direction, their parents sitting on the stairs to watch. The children living in the other half of the duplex at that time were Madge and Than Shaw, whose father, Professor Shaw, taught Italian at the university. My mother, always feeding my ambition, told me the professor enjoyed watching the games I made up. She told me he thought I would be an actress or go to university.

When we settled in Toronto our parents made the decision to send us to a private school. Immediately, one had to be dressed properly, books had to be bought, school lunches were put on the bill. Every month when that school account arrived, my mother would go over it groaning, saying that we'd have to cut out the extras, wondering if maybe last year's winter coat might still fit, if Sophie could wear my old tunic. My father seemed to take all this lightheartedly. On payday he handed out housekeeping money, and, presumably, he paid the rent and the Simpson's bill. But there seemed nothing my mother could do about emergencies: the doctor, the dentist, the plumber. It came to be that we felt guilty about asking her for things. We were supposed to get a weekly allowance, but often it was not forthcoming. If I simply had to have stockings or underwear, I was given a slip to go down to Simpson's and put it on the bill. I was never given the opportunity to budget or learn how to buy for myself.

In consequence, I think, I felt deprived, mean, drably dressed; the word *poor* became a real word. We were poor. And yet we lived in a middle-class neighbourhood and were supposed to be comfortably off. Although I continued to accept funds for my education, I felt "kept," and longed to earn my own living.

By the time I was at university, my father was earning a much larger salary as general manager of the Canadian Press, but it became evident that JFB always lived beyond his means and was often borrowing from the bank. Had my mother wanted to dress well and have her hair done occasionally, she never could have found the money, except for the manna from heaven that fell to her for some article she had written. It got so that she didn't try to keep herself in trim. All this while, my father gave us the impression, as his letters still show, that we could have anything we wanted. Thus we remained entirely dependent on JFB's generosity and were still innocents about spending and saving.

The one element in living that my father insisted on was good food; there was always meat or fish for dinner, several vegetables and a pie or pudding. It all depended on whether the current maid could cook. I remember coming into the kitchen once and finding Finnish Helmi in tears; she had been told to make a stuffing for the chicken, but when she looked in her dictionary she found the word *sage* meant *wise*. She did not know how to make a wise chicken for the Livesay family. Another girl was told to go down cellar and find the onions to make baked onions in white sauce, a favourite dish of JFB's. At dinner he plunged into them with gusto. "What a very peculiar taste!" he exclaimed. We all tasted. "They can't be onions," I said. Mother hastily called the cook and was taken down cellar to see where the girl had found the onions. What she had found were JFB's precious Dutch hyacinth bulbs waiting for spring. Even Scottish Mary, who certainly could speak English, had trouble with the strange vegetable she thought was "sparrow grass" (asparagus). This same Mary outdid herself in cleaning behind the bath – she moved it. The spurting pipes soon let us know. What a financial crisis when the plumber had to be called in!

It was small wonder that my parents sent me to a private girls' school rather than to the stream that would head for Harbord Collegiate. I would have an opportunity, they must have reasoned, to participate in the arts, and to get personal encouragement with writing. Besides, both my parents had been educated in private schools; their children must have the same opportunities.

The first school I was sent to, however, did not live up to expectations. It was the nearby St. Mildred's, run by Anglican sisters.

I fast became top of the class and teacher's pet, but there was no drama or music, and instead of outdoor basketball or skating I endured blue serge bloomers and dumbbells in the gymnasium. I did not make close friends and looked askance at my seatmate, who cheated during geography tests. At one point she seduced me into doing the same. When we both came out with perfect scores I was filled with hot shame and guilt. Never again would I do such a thing!

It was with fear and apprehension that I walked, the following September, down Spadina Avenue to Glen Mawr School. I had already met the principal, Miss Stuart, a formidable, stout English-woman who had been to Girton and who taught Greek and Latin. She wanted me to take both languages – I opted for Latin, but French instead of Greek. Later, I added German. As a matter of course we had English literature and grammar every day. A very dull book on geography, a Canadian history book, sewing and gymnastics made up the rest of our curriculum. The only bow to science was a weekly class of nature study in which we found and pressed flowers. Of course I had to take mathematics, as it was compulsory for senior matriculation.

Undoubtedly it was the freedom to enjoy rural life, which my parents accepted as a human right, that developed in me a love of solitude and induced a poetic sensibility. Soon after our settling in Toronto, my father purchased nine acres of woodland in Clarkson, Ontario. It was part of a two-hundred-acre pioneer farm and the land was called the woodlot. As time went on through the twenties, he started having a cottage built, which would later become one wing of a larger house. We went there all through the summer holidays and occasionally on weekends throughout spring and fall. The house was finally finished when I was abroad studying in Aix-en-Provence in 1930-31.

In the city, my father walked with us along the streets. At Woodlot, he usually gardened or pursued clouds with his camera. My sister and I were free to explore the woods on our own, and the dog went along joyfully, chasing rabbits. The treasured place in Clarkson for us was

Hammond's Wood, a valley below Erindale, where a small creek wound its way over stones. There might have been snake fences then, or barbed-wire fences for the cows, but we climbed over or crawled under these; there were no signs, as there are today, of "Trespassers Will Be Prosecuted" or "Private Property." We walked along the Credit River, or the shores of Lake Ontario, unimpeded. Mother, as I recall, never went for any real walks; she sauntered about over the grounds at Woodlot, looking for wildflowers, mushrooms and the birds that had been a part of her childhood in Compton, Quebec. In March, when the snow still lay on the ground, she instituted a miniature sugaring-off by boiling maple syrup and letting snow stiffen it until we could twist it around a fork. The early search for the first crocus on the Winnipeg prairie was transferred to the search for hepaticas and trilliums in the Ontario woods.

During my school years, attending a girls' school as a day student, I never had the opportunity to meet or to know boys. Indeed, I was painfully shy, tongue-tied and unable to find any way of communication. My father, perceiving how gauche and self-conscious I was, attempted to arrange social gatherings and doings for me with the twin sons of friends of his. How ridiculous I felt, trying to talk about boys' interests – sports, sports and sports, none of which I was good at. The gap between the sexes became even wider when the boys realized that I was a bluestocking, only interested in literature, music and the theatre. Worst of all, it was said that I wrote poetry! Had they seen my diary, they would have read these words: "It's a man's world."

JFB and I used to talk about all sorts of things when I was still an adolescent. He seemed to want to pass on his experiences. After supper he would call Paddy, our Irish terrier, pick up his walking stick and watch me as I put on my jacket against an autumn evening chill. Paddy would immediately seize the centre of the stick to show his prowess, keeping it balanced nearly all the way around the block. "Oh do stop and let him find a lamppost," I would demand. Father would chuckle,

"Let's see how long he can go without." Above all he admired tenacity, individual assertiveness, even in a dog.

As for his staff, I well knew that although he stressed pulling together, although he commanded and bullied, he had more than a sneaking appreciation for those men who stood up to him. On those half-hour walks around the tall brick duplex houses of the Annex, JFB would try to reveal to me his feelings about the young reporters and their lives, even to telling me of someone who had "got his girl in trouble." He was so sympathetic that he arranged for a transfer so that the young couple could move to a Canadian Press job in another city.

Strange that I did not wonder why he did not react as my mother and her family would have reacted, in typical Victorian fashion. I took it for granted that though he did not argue for free love, he implied that there was far too much fuss made about virginity; "It's so unrealistic," he said. Ironically, to prove his point, he gave me *Tess of the D'Urbervilles* to read. In such ways he cleared away my inhibitions long before I was ready to act on them.

My mother was an influence of the opposite kind. Once, looking through a volume of Michelangelo's prints my father had found in a secondhand store, she asked disgustedly: "What is so beautiful about nakedness? The human body is ugly, ugly!" As if to emphasize the fact, she wore shapeless clothes, her petticoat showed and her stockings seemed always to have runs. Slovenly, my father called her, to her face, and in front of us children.

A sense of family and individual conflicts dominated my teenage years in Toronto. It was only with my best friend, Gina, that I felt at ease, free to speak out my real feelings concerning the institutions of family, religion and capitalism, from all of which I longed to break free. My dream was to combine the childish belief in a fairy-tale Prince Charming who would rescue me, Cinderella, from the shackles of my life, with the mature desire for a purposeful feminist career as a novelist.

Parents: An Unarranged Marriage

Many are the ways of telling the truth. There is his way and her way and, now, my way. "How can I speak the truth?" my father cried out to me in near despair when he was forced to retire, through illness, and undertook a project, his newspaper memoirs. Because of his death, unfinished went these lively recollections of Canadian newspaper history. But my mother sorted through them and selected, cutting, snipping, pasting and, no doubt, burning. In the book published by the Ryerson Press in 1947, *The Making of a Canadian*, his truth became her truth. It was *her* telling, not his.

JFB's literary contribution up to that date was a book based on his news reports from the western front in 1917. Its title, *Canada's Hundred Days,* became a byword for those months of Canada's military glory. From the time of his appointment as general manager of the Canadian Press in Toronto around 1920 until his retirement in 1939, he was regarded as the organization's architect and builder. M. E. Nicholls, editor of the Vancouver *Province*, wrote of him: "He combined the elements of vision and executive capacity"; and I. Norman Smith of the Ottawa *Journal* wrote: "He had contributed to the national cohesion of Canada more than any one man of his generation." In a letter to me, one of JFB's staff members, Leon Edel (now a renowned critic), made the following assessment:

JFB was a very alert and sensitive man, and I remember how he responded to certain news stories which I wrote, and caught certain sensitivities of observation and phrase, which he underlined in memoranda to the more literal minded members of his staff — a news agency has to have such. But it was his appreciation of my way of looking at things that warmed me to him, his subtle verbal mind; and then we had our common interest in [Henry] James.

He was a man of unusual sensitivity to head up the kind of organization that must handle news often in such a cut and dried way. Certainly he managed to make it lively and he was a splendid administrator.

However, it was because JFB knew so well all the leading journalists and publishers in Canada that he found it difficult to write of his experiences. After all, his friends (and enemies?) were still alive. He did, however, finish his travel essays, which recorded delightful visits to Peggy's Cove. These, accompanied by photographs taken on his trips, were published by the Ryerson Press soon after his death in 1944.

What was true or false about my father's childhood, his lost youth, his delay in marrying? Right up to the end: what was true about his death?

In the book of memoirs he was editing before he died on June 15, 1944, my father described in glowing terms his early childhood in Ventnor, Isle of Wight, and at Rosturk Castle, County Mayo, Ireland. His childless aunt there, Emily Bligh Vesey-Stoney, decided to adopt one of the eleven children of her sister Sophy, who had married John Livesay and was living in Ventnor. The boy chosen to go to Rosturk "on trial" was John Frederick Bligh, known as Fred, aged about seven. After a year, he was sent home in disgrace; he believed it was because he had stolen some jam! After that experience, he began to stammer badly and had a rough and ready time of it with bullying older brothers who used him, he told me, in more ways than one. His comfort was in his sister Ina and in his gentle poetry-writing and music-loving mother. Sophy was pious and wrote hymns, but played Chopin on the piano; the religious tracts she wrote she stuffed into the fishermen's lobster pots. He was so close to her he called her by her first name. And because she had been born in Ireland, in County Meath, JFB never lost interest in the Irish connection and the Bligh family.

JFB's maternal grandfather, Charles Bligh, had been one of those Anglo-Irish settlers in Dublin who came under the influence of John Nelson Darby, founder of the Plymouth Brethren. This fundamentalist sect had spread from Plymouth to Dublin, and Sophy Bligh and her sister, Emily, were reared in that faith. Edmund Gosse's autobiography, *Father and Son*, describes what such a family was like; for JFB, who finally rebelled against it, "There was something deep and Christ-like in their simple faith."

Charles Bligh moved his family from Ireland to Ventnor and it was there his daughter Sophy met a young architect, John Livesay, in the Meeting House. Eventually, Livesay's professional interest caused him to clash with those of the faith; he became the renegade who designed fanciful Gothic gables for Ventnor's new housing and, worse, he built a theatre! Further, he was an alcoholic, a lover of display and of cadging to aristocracy. JFB's memory of his father, my grandfather whom I never met, is vivid:

If he never drew a sober breath in those days, it is only fair to say such was the case with 90% of the voters, for beer flowed freely in the taverns, in the committee rooms and under the very nose of the returning officer and his deputies. My father was popular among his fellows and I never heard of his being drunk in a public place. He kept that for home and the midnight watch. He did not smoke and never swore. But to his sons it was: "Hold out your hand, sir!" and crash would come the architect's rule, a sadistic vent to his feelings.

The published version of my father's memoirs scarcely reveals the discordances of his childhood years. True, he gives a dark picture of his father's ruthlessness with his sons, but he paints a charming portrait of his mother. The pain that he really endured, internally, as a sensitive, introspective adolescent, was balanced by his long walks over the Downs, by his great love of the outdoors, of the sea and sailing, and by his keen mind, deeply interested in politics. Since he so loved the sea, he remembered,

I was crazy to enter the Navy – and when it developed at thirteen that the usual channel was closed because of my stammering, my father secured a special nomination from Lord George, First Lord of the Admiralty....I took remedial stammering lessons, but they only made me more self-conscious, and when I came before the special Board at Portsmouth, it was hopeless from the start.

The ensuing years seem to have been spent at school in Ryde, where the boy Fred showed a great aptitude for history. He wanted to go to London University, but again his way was blocked. Grandfather Bligh's money had seemingly run out. The alternative was emigration to the colonies. Fred decided to take a cattle boat to Canada, like so many young Englishmen around 1900, with his youngest brother, Charles. At least they knew there were relatives there, on the Bligh side, who would welcome them with open arms. He has described those years as follows:

Although we descended out of the blue on the Canadian household in which we found ourselves, it was most hospitable to the two greenhorns. Charles left after a month. In scorching summers (notwithstanding all the kindness I received) I was often ready to slip away and weep, longing for rain, clouds and the Downs – lonely and homesick for my own people and my sea.

In the early 1900s young JFB tried prospecting in Ontario and harvesting in Saskatchewan, at the same time writing for both English and Canadian periodicals. At the age of twenty-eight he took his first full-time newspaper job, which was with the Regina *Standard*. When

J. F. B. Livesay, 1912

he moved to a better position on the Winnipeg *Telegram*, he met his wife-to-be, Florence Randal. After a long up-and-down courtship, these two, in their midthirties, plunged into marriage in 1908. Some semblance of economic security lay ahead, for JFB had been appointed, in 1907, as manager of the newly formed news-gathering cooperative, the Western Associated Press. In 1917 this association merged with three eastern Canada news cooperatives; thus the Canadian Press, as we know it today, was formed.

What JFB really endured during his early years in Canada is revealed to me in letters dated 1930, a time of retrospective regret concerning his unfulfilled creativity and his frustrating marriage:

What you never realize is that we — the older generation — us, I, JFBL, at your age went through exactly the same turmoil of ambition and endeavour you are in. I was set on literary fame and had not a chance — just plain wasting — absolutely wasting — 17 to 19 in Ventnor, sterile and debasing and 20 to 29 in Canada, farming, etc., literally devouring it ravenously, and bit so hard and deep I could never let go or get back to spiritual things. I used to think I could someday write of those tragic barren years — the caged starling — but I know I will die in this harness, a not unworthy employ.

And the crown of my achievement is that both Sophie and you can go your ways — your artistic ways — without my snout-sniffling in barren lands. So you see I can sympathize. P.S. Your poor mother never had an aspiration beyond pretty-pretty.

That letter, and several others written to me in Aix, reveal the beginning of the rift with his wife, his inability to cope with the loss of his children's unalloyed allegiance, and his downhill road through an impossible love affair to physical though not mental breakup. In his final years of retirement, he did display considerable insight, as the following passage reveals; regarding his inner life, let this be the last word:

The two prime factors in my life were stammering and alcohol, so this is the story of a struggle, a fight. There were girls; girls are more forward than boys – one didn't know what to do with them; but stammering cut off the sex. For many years, stammering cut me off from even knowing the people next door.

The little boy of seven, in Ireland, was fluent. One of my most vivid memories is that of a boy of six or seven spinning yarns for the butler in my aunt's house, fairy tales, so evidently someone came near enough to get through the stammering; but it is worth recalling, because through the technique one developed, it became an offensive weapon.

Alcohol – in my father's life and my own. Looking back, it seems a long fight against alcohol, but then a sense of proportion is lost. One remembers rather the vales and peaks of alcoholic depression – the misery of it – I have felt like suicide many times. It was a fashionable failing in my family. But there was a pride that carried one on.

The idea was latent in one's youth but very definite in all those years of failure of which I have spoken. It was easier to shoot one's self, but I could not hurt my mother. And yet was it so easy? When one looked down the barrel, one was afraid to pull the trigger. But this business of looking in upon yourself can be quite terrible. Even after fifty years, life and experience lack point; yet there are some hilltops that still stand, some descents to the valley that still obscure the moving spirit.

It is terribly difficult to be honest with one's self when one knows too much, life becomes difficult – yet in these notes I will try to be honest and fair, as becomes a newspaper man.

✒

My mother, Florence Hamilton Randal, was the middle girl of three, with three much younger brothers. She was born on November 3, 1874, in Compton, Quebec, a part of the English enclave known as the Eastern Townships, which had been settled largely by United Empire Loyalists from New England. Florence spoke and understood French because her mother, a semi-orphan, had been sent to a French convent school in St-Hyacinthe. My grandmother, Mary Louisa Andrews, was considered to be well educated in French, music and the household arts. In Compton, she married Stephen Randal, whose father, also Stephen, had been a teacher of classics in the Talbot Seminary, St. Thomas, Ontario, and a journalist with the Hamilton *Free Press*.

Times were hard in the small village of Compton, where the French and English lived in harmony, side by side. My grandfather became a shopkeeper, housepainter and real estate agent. He did not enjoy good health and died of Parkinson's disease when Florence was only fourteen. Somehow, the widow, Mary Louisa Randal, managed to feed her family from the vegetable garden and to keep a cow and chickens. A well-to-do Andrews uncle supplied the family with a slaughtered pig or a barrel of molasses, and of course the mother baked her own bread. As for the education of the three Randal daughters, an Anglican Church school, Compton Ladies' College, came to their rescue. There were always free places at the school for the clergyman's daughters, but since the incumbent had none, those places were given to the Randal girls. They therefore received a good education in English, French and music, and they wrote their provincial examinations.

The youngest girl, Kathleen, was interested in housekeeping and helping her mother with the vegetable garden, cow and chickens. The oldest, Helen, was very clever at school but knew from the start that she would have to go out into the world and make her own way. Helen did her best getting positions as nurse-governess, but her great desire was to train as a nurse at the Royal Victoria Hospital in Montreal. Eventually she managed it. Florence then took Helen's place as governess at the Sequin School for Backward Children in New York.

At seventeen, my mother found teaching arduous, with little time left for herself. She also had few friends with whom to enjoy the pleasures of the city. The following year she returned to Montreal, where she began teaching in a position she enjoyed, and later she became a special teacher of Latin and French at Buckingham Public School, Quebec. It was during this period of her life that the signature *Florence Hamilton Randal* was to be found in a Montreal weekly under the column "Character Sketches and Verses" and in 1896 her name appeared in the prestigious *Massey's Magazine* of Toronto. Stories and poems by her were published alongside those of Charles G. D. Roberts and Archibald Lampman.

How was it that she was so spurred on not only to write, but to get published? The emphasis at home had been on gentility, churchgoing and a high moral standard insisted upon by the matriarch, my witty but stern grandmother. Because Mary Louisa Randal was also a staunch Tory, newspapers were read and talked about. Probably at school, where Florence excelled in French and English, she had access to books and magazines. It seems clear she was writing stories and verses at an early age. Strangely enough, FRL never talked to me about that youthful writing, or to what degree she was encouraged, or by whom. Not by the Randal family, certainly, for the attitude of her brothers was that their sister's writing was a joke, and the family was suspicious of intellectuals. Perhaps, however, my grandmother had talked about my mother's paternal grandfather, the first Stephen Randal, that journalist in Hamilton, Ontario.

Undoubtedly it would have been pointed out to Florence that she could never, as a woman, hope to earn a living by writing poetry and stories, so she turned to journalism, sending out sketches to the Montreal *Standard* and the Ottawa *Journal*. Finally, her chance came for a position on the *Journal* as society editor. In those early days of Canadian journalism, shorthand was an asset, and FRL had also learned to type. Then too, her attractive appearance must have played a large part in the placement, which involved attending government social events and reporting on engagements and weddings. Her features were delicate and flowerlike. A fine, near perfect nose took one's attention away from a rather large mouth. In every other respect, she was small and well proportioned. For those reasons men were immediately attracted to her, but few of them ever satisfied her ideal of a husband who would offer her intellectual companionship far above the demands of the flesh. She had been reared by women and was at a loss with men, not knowing how to deal with them other than as pals.

FRL's diaries painfully reveal her innocence as well as her keen interest in analyzing character. In those days it was the custom for young men coming into the cities for work to live in boarding houses. The young women who followed this pattern must have been few and far between, but FRL found herself such a niche. Her Ottawa diary for 1902 records some of the social life of that period. She seems to have met important and interesting people like Marconi and Charles Gibson and his wife, the original Gibson girl.

It is to be noted that although the young ladies of the day were often "fagged," as soon as there was the possibility of a dance they revived amazingly. Florence not only danced, skated and played ping-pong, she also sang, accompanying herself on the piano, and recited at social gatherings.

The accomplishments that FRL never achieved were housekeeping and cooking, for her boarding-house life continued right through her working years. And, suddenly, at the age of twenty-seven, her chance came to travel and see the world. In March 1902, the Boer War was coming to a close and England decided that the Dutch children of the Transvaal must learn English. Thirty Canadian teachers were offered places, including my mother. Everyone in Ottawa seems to have been excited about this, but FRL had a more realistic idea of what she was getting into:

Went to a little tea at Mrs. Green's. Every one is saying such nice things about me that I think some of them at least must be true, and that they have liked my work on the Journal. *Of course I hope to come back and (or) will do so — although the gossips have all decided that I am to be married out there. It is all considered "so romantic" and "so interesting." For my part I don't expect a picnic by any means, but I do hope I shall be able to write back good letters.*

After a stormy trip to England, followed by a Cook's tour of London, the Canadian contingent found themselves on shipboard again, on an idyllic and fascinating voyage to South Africa where shipboard flirtations with young officers were a hint of things to come. The ship landed at Cape Town, then the Canadian teachers were moved to the Transvaal. On June 1, at Camp Irene near Pretoria, they heard the hoped-for news. The headmaster called the teachers and staff into the drawing-room tent and proclaimed that peace had been achieved; Florence's sympathy was with the Boer teachers on staff. My mother then plunged into the duties of teaching, combined with journalism, as she was sending articles to the Ottawa *Journal*.

By the new year, 1903, the teaching centres began to be broken up. Those girls who would agree to sign a contract for three years were assigned teacherages in farm camps, some distance from any city. FRL decided not to stay beyond her one year, though the pay was good. She was losing her close friend Nan Moulton, and she could not make up her mind about Wackie, a young British officer who kept "proposing." What her diaries don't say, but what is implicit, is that FRL was homesick. Although twenty-eight now, she had never freed herself from her mother's help in all major decisions. She had been told so often that she was frail and delicate that it would seem she came to believe it. Sick headaches, probably migraines, and colds kept up with her in South Africa; and perhaps most important of all, but never admitted, she had failed to find that dream husband. So she returned in April of 1903 to Canada, bent more consciously now on having a holiday at home and then finding work.

A year later, FRL didn't have any trouble getting established in Winnipeg:

I saw Premier Roblin and got assurances of future work, but meantime I had heard of a nice position, as a sort of Private Secretary to Mr. Sanford Evans, of the Telegram, *and thinking there would be more chances of advancement there and knowing that it would be congenial work, I began with him on*

Nov.28.03. Except for the confinement of the long afternoons, the routine has been easy and pleasant enough. I had a few little South African sketches printed, and I hope later to do extra writing, as $43 a month, while a good payment for what I am doing, is not enough.

Of these times, this description from the diaries fits best:

Three years ago today the Queen died. I don't seem to feel much like writing in a diary these days. I have so little in my private life to write about. I have just been reading over last year at this time. Was it only last year that I sat on a moonlit verandah in South Africa and listened to all sorts of things?

As if to challenge the climate, however, there was more going on in Winnipeg than in a colonial setting. Not only skating parties, dances, private musical evenings and restaurant dining in the handsome palm-fringed Mariaggi's, where the newspaper crowd flocked after the theatre, but every week saw travelling companies bringing the current plays and concerts from New York or even London. It is interesting to note the mélange of great performers, actors and singers who came to Winnipeg, usually with sentimental, frothy stock-company theatricals. FRL, as the secretary to the publisher of the Winnipeg *Telegram*, began to reveal her talents as a reporter. She was given interviews with important visitors to the city, as well as concerts and plays to review. With her friend Nan Moulton, now returned to Canada, she saw Sarah Bernhardt in *Camille*, remarking that "we understood scarcely a word, but enjoyed it just the same." She saw Harold Nelson in *Hamlet*, "scarcely a first-class performance, but as I had never seen it before I was interested." She preferred seeing *Resurrection*, "a story play, if not a very pleasant one." The D'Oyly Carte Company came to Winnipeg, as well as light opera and vaudeville.

On February 8 of 1904, war broke out between Russia and Japan. Amid all this excitement, recorded in her diary, FRL also managed to remember:

A year ago tonight I was sitting on a moonlit steppe while Tom's eyes told me what his lips did later in the little mess room — as he cried out against his long enforced silence. It's a contrast indeed with tonight — the little rented bedroom where I sit and write after the day in the office — and no one to care whether I am alone or not. But it was best to go from him since I did not care. And I fancy he has consoled himself since.

As is indicated by her diary entry for February 29 – "This is the day that comes so seldom that it needs to be written on. My article is out in the March *Canadian* and looks well, I think." – my mother continued to write, not giving up her ambition. At the same time, she was enjoying a repetition of the South African pattern of playing games with admirers. These were Mr. Beaufort and Mr. Livesay:

Mr. Beaufort gave me a lovely bunch of jonquils today. With him and with Mr. Livesay I am getting to be quite friendly. There is a sort of semi-rivalry with them to talk to me if both are around. Usually it's a case of Box and Cox, and Cox doesn't know how Box fares or vice versa. Livesay the other day undertook to carve my initials on my pencil. When finished they read "F.R.L." But of course he just loves a quiet bit of flirting.

When May came, however, Mr. Livesay seemed to be winning out. He invited her to go canoeing and he was always bringing her books. They sat under the trees in a hammock. By the end of May, FRL wrote: "Mr. Livesay has given an agreeable tinge to my days in the *Telegram*, which would have been dull without his badinage. We are good comrades now, and I like him." She was obviously very attracted to him:

He likes me well enough to find me amusing and he interests me with his raillery and clever repartee, so it's quite satisfactory all around. He lent me The Letters of Horace Walpole *and I have enjoyed them ever so much.*

FRL was about this time beginning to do more interviews. Her great success at the office came when she interviewed an actor named Laurence D'Arcy. "The foreman of the printers – and this was considered the greatest compliment – swore roundly, 'That girl can write!' " But all the while she was struggling to do freelance journalism, she was also seeking to please the man whom she began to call her "literary conscience." JFB Livesay kept bringing her books to read to round out her education. He was often away on assignments in the west, and of one such occasion she wrote, "Do not miss him as much as I thought as I am very busy nearly all day marking editorials and I am supposed to do the book page for a time."

The couple had been observed by someone in the office and that resulted in gossip and "smiles and significant glances" that had not existed before. "I suppose it had to come sooner or later," she wrote, "but I have been so careful in the office." FRL was not only frustrated in her literary friendship, but also in doubt about marriage versus career. She realized that she was thirty years old, a spinster, and had made little mark as a writer. She confessed:

It's so tiresome to have a little literary ability that will never amount to anything and yet hounds one out of laissez faire. I never had any pretension to ability above the usual run of people "with a gift" for that sort of thing and yet there comes so often the sense of failure – not in my usual work, for I don't slight that. I suppose it's really lack of persistent effort – I'm too much a dilettante and don't honestly care much for general applause as long as a few know that I have done a little that was good.

During that autumn of 1904, FRL dismissed her concerns about writing and a career because she was preoccupied with her relationship with JFB. She was continuously saying things like "have been lazy about writing"; "it has been dull and lonely"; "my old chats with Mr. Livesay a thing of the past. I miss them a good deal but fortunately not as much as I might."

The year 1905 opened more hopefully for my mother. The weather was unusually mild that winter and the two "swains" who jostled for her attention were increasingly attentive: Mr. Beaufort, "Beau," and Mr. Livesay, "Live." It was clear that the first one was madly in love, but was held at arm's length by FRL, whereas Live was ambivalent, sometimes ready to give her intellectual stimulus on a chums level, sometimes quelling her hopes by mentioning other lady loves or just being plain difficult:

We quarrelled today – "The Philanderer" and I – over some trivial matter in the office. He was rude and I thought that before this I had overlooked it often enough. It's his unfortunate manner, of course, but it's about time he learnt not to vent his bad temper on everyone. And anyway, a coolness prevents the other thing.

Later, although the affair seemed to be coming to a happy conclusion, there was another setback:

Mr. Livesay and I were to have gone out canoeing today, but instead, as he informed me he had no money we went out into the country for a ramble. We nearly quarrelled before I went out so it was scarcely as happy a day as it might have been, but I wasn't altogether sorry I had gone. He has told me all about his various and sundry "girls." He confesses that he isn't in love with anyone, but yet is anxious to settle down. He is a nice fellow and I like him, but if I were married to a man like him I'd want him to care, for otherwise I think he'd be very selfish.

At times, FRL did some honest self-searching. Throughout 1905 and 1906, during what came to be a most exasperating courtship, FRL was nonetheless doing some of her own writing and sending it out to Canadian magazines. She needed encouragement and recorded,

Two years ago today I came to Winnipeg. I'm afraid I haven't accomplished much in that time, though in the office they think I can write. And I think they

like me pretty well. Mrs. Evans said I had helped her husband ever so much,
but I don't know that I have.

In October of 1906, my mother had come to an important decision:
she had decided to resign from her job at the *Telegram* because they had
insisted that she be part secretary and part women's editor. She was
sorry about giving up, but there seemed no way of arranging a
compromise. Instead, she was finding encouragement for her freelance
writing. She received her first cheque for an article about the
Mormons in an English magazine; I wonder if she told this to my
father, or whether she hugged her success to herself.

By the beginning of the year 1907, FRL, the patient Griselda, was
still putting up with neglect and silences on the part of Live, her
wandering newspaperman. She wrote on March 25: "It worries me
that he doesn't write" and then later, "Heard at last and he seems to
think that no explanation is needed *between friends*."

The next diary entry is two months later. On May 24, FRL had
received an offer of marriage:

Today Arthur and I went out to River Park. When we came back I answered
Live's letter and told him that some day I would take the job of looking after
him. I can hardly believe that the story has come true after all.

On October 25 my father was introduced to my mother's family, then
living in Winnipeg at 116 Polson Avenue. My grandmother had
moved from Compton in the Eastern Townships to keep house with
her daughter Kathleen and son Arthur. The latter, FRL's devoted
younger brother, never accepted her choice of husband. Perhaps the
strangest reticence on FRL's part was the fact that she never recorded
or mentioned JFB's stammer. Instead of discussing this severe handicap
with her mother, she recorded only: "He's very reserved and does not
show at his best and I think Mother was a little disappointed."

By November 1907, the engaged couple were seeing each other,
but they were not thinking of immediate marriage. Several times a

Florence Randal Livesay at Lake of the Woods, ca. 1916

week they had tea and played cards. All the little gaieties had to be given up as JFB was finding it hard to manage on his small salary. Through all this, FRL didn't worry about getting married by Christmas, although JFB "practically hypnotized her into saying she would."

The lack of money persisted, and my mother's diary entry for December 25 reads:

Weather turned suddenly very cold. I went to Christ Church but found the service very long. Mother was able to enjoy her dinner. In the evening I went to Janet's for tea. Live telephoned but I knew he wanted to be by himself today as he is still very blue.

December 29:

We went for Christmas dinner, as of old, to Fergie's. But this time it was not the same as in the old days. Live and I almost quarrelled over a misunderstanding and the walk home was dreadful. Today he was very patient. It took it out of both of us a lot.

There are no further entries in my mother's diary until this one:

August 31st, 1908 – After all there is only to be this one entry for all these months and the things that have been will never be written down here. Tomorrow is my wedding day – the 39th anniversary of Mother's wedding. It doesn't seem a bit real of course, but the little brown house among the oaks is very much real. Today at the office they gave me such a lovely gift – the dear kind people whom I hope I shall never leave wholly – a mahogany desk chair and china tea set. Mother has been like a brick all through things. It's lovely having her here. If all goes well tomorrow at three o'clock in St. John's Cathedral Live and I will be married. I am writing it down to make it seem real, for working up at the office until the very last has made any change in my life seem impossible. I do hope and pray we shall be happy and that I can be the woman he needs for all his soul-sides as well as everyday things.

They spent their honeymoon in a borrowed cottage at Whytewold on Lake Winnipeg.

During that first year of marriage, before I appeared on the scene, FRL kept up her freelance writing and her guided reading program. Both she and JFB were extremely interested in the Canadian poetry of Roberts, Lampman and D. C. Scott. It is clear that in the early years of their marriage, when my sister, Sophie, and I were toddlers, there was an intellectual exchange of ideas between my parents that was more important to them than the difficulties lying dormant: her Victorian prudery and his sophisticated European romanticism, which ran counter to his own strict Plymouth Brethren upbringing.

At that time – the second decade of the century – Winnipeg was a stimulating town and newspaper reporters were in the centre of it, having access to all the cultural entertainments, the travelling actors, singers and distinguished lecturers who came for one-night stands. In addition, for my mother there was the Winnipeg Women's Press Club where she met some fascinating feminist friends – Cora Hind, Kennethe Haig, Valance Patriarche, Ruth Cohen – and where Nellie McClung and Emily Murphy (Janey Canuck) were already legendary. Through the efforts of the two latter women, Manitoba in 1916 became the first Canadian province to grant women the vote.

In the 1920s the stresses between my parents became more marked. Mother often considered divorce, but in those days if a woman left home she had no recourse. She might take the children, but she would have no income. Legally, she was nowhere; so divorce was out. I think it would have been very traumatic for me, and probably for my younger sister, too, had FRL divorced my father. Nonetheless, it might have cleared up the growing antagonism between them if they had been separated. Sophie and I might have had a better chance to know each parent in their own realm, rather than in the household with all the bickering.

My most painful time concerning my parents' marriage was when I was still a schoolgirl. During one of his drinking binges, JFB knocked my mother down. She fled to a neighbour's with Sophie and called Mr. Tibbs of the Canadian Press to come over and handle her husband. She left me alone with him. I remember coming downstairs in my nightgown to where JFB sat by the fire. This would have been when we lived on Rosemount Avenue. Stuttering, he began talking about his feelings, his aims, I suppose his attachment to us girls and so on. At one point he embraced me fiercely. I did not consciously analyze the embrace, but as I look back on it, it was not a sexual advance; it was just the agony of a man utterly frustrated in his emotional life. The doorbell rang and Mr. Tibbs came in and sat with him for the rest of the night.

JFB's bouts of alcoholism occurred only every six months, because he definitely had periods when he said, "I'm going on the water wagon," and he did. After these bouts of two or three days drinking, he would sober up and collapse. But he collapsed into bed with sciatica, so Mother had to phone the office and say he was ill and couldn't come in. All this was very upsetting, I think, to us as girls, specially as he often lost his temper over small things. I remember one night being wakened up by the sound of an altercation in the street between my father and a taxi driver. I was so embarrassed by this that I didn't walk to school the normal way at all, but went along back lanes in case I met anyone who also had been wakened in the night and heard my father.

It is surprising, and worth recording, that when JFB was found to be diabetic as well as suffering from heart disease, he did completely stop drinking.

My parents did not share their twenties; they were totally unknown to each other then, living different lives. When they met in their early thirties they became again different people to each other and their separate pasts – their childhoods, adolescences and twenties – were something they could not share. But the relationship started on the newspaper had been that of the brilliant man who was the teacher and the ambitious young woman who was the pupil.

JFB must have seen in FRL the potential for a warm mother for a brood of boys, manager of a household, cook, seamstress, comforter. Instead, he had hit upon the one of the three Randal daughters who was in an unacknowledged revolt against the woman's place in the home. A woman who, after leaving boarding school at seventeen, had struck out for herself, teaching and reporting, and was geared to great ambitions. She was spirited, creative, thirsty for any knowledge, any books JFB could give her. Perhaps this is why my father called my mother "a bag of tricks," meaning mentally and spiritually. Sometimes she was yielding, and sometimes she had a stubborn will of her own. She kept him guessing, and that must have been the variety of stimuli he needed.

The concept of wife as helpmeet was strong in the days at the beginning of the century. Yet my mother had refused to say the word "obey" in the Anglican marriage service. She would love and honour but not obey her husband. As a student, I admired her for having taken this stand, but I saw, all too clearly, that every day she was obliged to subscribe to her husband's needs.

My mother was torn between her very traditional, conservative, provincial, Protestant upbringing and her desire to become a person in her own right; my father was an emigrant drifter who rejected the old world and sought a new start in a democratic society where women would be the equal of men and where there was no shame in being called a radical, one who goes to the root of things. Live's frustrations developed from the conflict between his idealism and the raw individualism, the jockeying for power in the Canadian newspaper world. Faced with having to support a wife and two children at home, and with building a news service that showed a profit, he became more and more authoritarian: a traditional father figure to whom his children and his staffers were expected to look for guidance.

What seems clear to me now is that these two people should not have married. During their courtship, my mother wrote about being Live's pal and how they were not destined to marry. Eventually, she recorded how she thought he had hoped they could be married chums because she wasn't sexually aroused. On the other hand, it is perfectly clear that she was very much in love with him, although he treated her in a most offhand, tantalizing, macho way. Whenever he came close, they seemed to be in harmony, but then he would start telling her about another girl with whom he was in love. This situation, as it develops in the diary, is really painful. FRL once wrote, "I should have been a nun, I'm so unresponsive to the sex thing."

How ironic it is that my father persisted in thinking all his married life that my mother was not a virgin when he married her. To me she confided how, years later, in a fit of vituperation he told her of the shock of his wedding night: he was convinced she was not a virgin. Yet I am sure that she was perfectly honest in telling me he was wrong. She was not a passionate woman; she was beautiful to look at, but uninterested in sex. She liked men for their intellectual stimulus and because they flattered her. I have no doubt, on the other hand, that my father was in love with my mother at the beginning of their marriage. But my mother's account of the honeymoon breakfast is significant: "He went out to the kitchen to make ham and eggs for our breakfast, and for the first time I heard how he could swear. It made me feel quite sick." When my sister and I were teenagers, JFB told us, as a naughty boy would tell it: "She came to me with nothing! On our honeymoon I even had to buy her a pair of pants." So they stuck needles in one another; JFB, I fear, with much more malice than his wife. She never accepted the fact, visible to everyone else, that he resented her, sometimes intensely. Yet he could not do without her. She ran his house, in a sort of way, although in his retirement he engaged a housekeeper to do the rough work. Most importantly, though, FRL gave him two children. He simply adored children.

Belief and Unbelief

"Never trust a person with brown eyes," my father pronounced. Yet later he was charmed by my young friend Gina and her brown eyes. However, I was beginning to be concerned about adult prejudices, and this remark of JFB's was perturbing. I had not read any anthropology at that stage, nor any history of the origins of humankind, but I wondered that a green-eyed Englishman should cast doubt on the honesty of Spaniards and Italians, not to mention the peoples of Asia and Africa. JFB would often come out with misconceptions of this sort, without thinking. It was as if he had, at English boarding school, absorbed other boys' gossip and taken it as truth, never again to be questioned. Strange, when he questioned everything else.

My diary for 1927 expressed my feelings this way:

1. My mother, most persistent of Christians, says: the white race must survive, because it is infinitely superior to any other race.
2. My father, a diligent reader of history, declares: war is a necessity of nature; war must be.
3. And they both agree with each other.

For myself, I gave the word *intolerance* a new meaning: that of questioning parental ideas. So I commented: "I find it very easy, very splendid to be intolerant. The word seethes in my mind, intolerance! Infinitely better than self-satisfaction."

When I was a high-school girl, my father and I had many lively discussions after supper. One evening, I remember particularly the conversation turned to Meredith's *The Egoist,* which JFB had recently given me to read. He wanted my reaction. I was then in the throes of being prepared for confirmation at St. Alban's, the Anglican cathedral, and of pondering the message of the catechism and the gospel.

"I don't think it's good to think only of yourself, and proclaim your ideas above others," I told him.

"Nonsense," he replied. "The only interesting people are those who express their individuality."

"You are always running down people who are bores. Why? They can't help it."

"I've no use for a man or woman who hasn't developed any intelligence he or she may have – any individuality."

"Yet when you meet such people – or live with them, like Mother – you put them down."

"We won't talk about your mother."

But, alas, we were a family that did talk about each other, did analyze sometimes quite cruelly. So I was torn between respecting my mother's emotional attachment to Christianity and conservatism and my father's agnosticism. "I am a radical," he would proclaim. "One who goes to the roots of things." Each parent sought to reign over me.

Actually, I was attached to the Anglican liturgy, the language of the King James version of the prayer book and the Bible. I never knew what it was to have a religious experience, but I loved the aesthetics of the church, the intoned psalms whose language was pure poetry. But there was another, less noble element to my churchgoing. Looking back now I would dub myself a church snob, because each week during Lent I recorded, for my Sunday school teacher, the number of times I had been to church. And before being confirmed, my class-mates and I had to memorize the catechism, for which there was a prize. That year I won the prize for perfect performance. A five-dollar gold piece. (This I treasured and had with me several years later when

I went to study in Provence; "In case of emergency," I told my mother. The emergency developed at Aix: a toothache and a tooth filling required for which I had no ready cash. The gold coin was rung down on the teller's desk and declared viable. The dentist did the rest. By that time I had forgotten the answers in the catechism.)

It was after being confirmed and receiving communion that I was disturbed because, try to concentrate as I would, I had no sensation of having been changed by receiving the Body and Blood, the bread and wine. I began to feel hypocritical. What was the use of getting up early, early, on a Sunday morning, while others overslept, slipping silently out of the house without breakfast and walking through Toronto's deserted streets to communion service at St. Alban's? Certainly it was a time of peace and meditation, but I gained no spiritual solace from it. My epiphanies occurred in the woods, at Clarkson. A summary of these experiences appears in a diary notation:

Feeling myself, in cleansing moments of humility only an instrument, a vessel; feeling this, I know that it is the Creative Force that drives the universe. Men call sex life's most dominant force: but what is sex save an expression of creation? Yes, yes: I have cried Glory! when I was swayed by this great power; I have known, I know. God is Creative Force; perhaps even He is less than that, an instrument, a perfect or imperfect (who shall say) vessel of the one true vitality, Creation.

I was then beginning to abandon formal religion and the church structure. Several people were responsible for my questioning: Gina, whose reading in scientific and anthropological literature far outstripped mine, and more especially my father, because of his agnosticism. These thoughts I kept to myself, but an event at Sunday school brought the questioning into sharp focus.

My friend in the class, Audrey, shared with me a devotion to our teacher, Miss Morris. Before and during confirmation we became so fond of her that we asked the superintendent if our class could continue to have her next year, instead of being promoted to a regular Bible class. But this gentle woman, single, probably in her thirties, who had been such a support to us when we were fourteen, was unable to cope with our maturing minds at fifteen or sixteen. We were by then following a course of study on the history of the Reformation and the formation of the Church of England following Henry VIII's break with the Pope. Our teacher took the view that the Church of England was the direct descendant of the early Christian communities. "How can that be," I asked, "when the Roman Catholic Church is descended from St. Peter and we are a breakaway from that church?" Miss Morris was unable either to understand my question or to answer it. On the following Sunday she was not present as teacher, and then we heard through Bible class members that she was ill in hospital.

What to do? Audrey and I decided it would be right to visit Miss Morris. No one prevented us, and there was no one present in the small private room where our teacher lay, strangely listless. She would begin to talk, and then suddenly her face would crumple up and twitch, her eyes rolling. Audrey and I lowered our eyes and dared not even look at each other. To our relief, the contractions stopped long enough for us to say we hoped she'd be better, but we had to go now. We ran down the corridor to the stairs, and once outside the hospital we were gasping, "Oh. Oh. Whatever can be the matter?"

Some months later we heard that Miss Morris was out of hospital, but that she wouldn't be back at Sunday school. She had joined the Salvation Army. That is when it dawned on me that my precocious questions may have shaken her faith, and led to a nervous breakdown. I never knew for sure, but the sense of guilt haunted me.

It must have been the following summer that I had long midnight talks with Gina, who often was permitted to come to Woodlot to visit. She was by this time a confirmed atheist, deep in newfound scientific knowledge, for she was taking courses that would admit her into medicine. My mother was most resentful of this influence, and made a great effort to "save my faith" by having Canon Seaman of St. Alban's

Cathedral talk to me. She knew that I thought him a fine type of man. However, the canon sent his wife to our Walmer Road house for tea. FRL must have left us alone, but I cannot remember anything except a feeling of acute embarrassment.

I recorded my new state in my journal, following a literary gathering to which the Canadian Authors' Association had invited me:

So, this is a bitter gift. A gift of aloneness. All those people last night – E. J. Pratt, Pelham Edgar, Mazo de la Roche – they did not see. They have not reached the bottom of themselves. They know not pity.

Honesty between people is impossible. It does not exist, I think, in any society. It is mockery to say that word. In that grey anguish I found no need for "everlasting life." What I have argued, I now feel. So all is well. I am a sort of atheist, in that I believe God is in nature: that he was the beginning. But there have been too many men on this earth, and too many worlds, for me to conceive of a personal god. It is more beautiful, perhaps, but a false comfort. No man can say, I know. And to say, I believe, is to deliberately blind oneself.

O I am filled with mockery; it is not good. But to have a clear vision of people you must be without emotion. And that leads to a hardening, a malice of the senses. There is only the mind left.

Unconscious irony. What I was discovering was what my father had been saying to me all along.

Gina

Ah, Gina, is it only after seventy years of living that I begin to understand you? We met when we were about twelve, in the spring of 1921. The place was Clarkson, Ontario, a small village on the highway between Toronto and Hamilton. Both your parents and mine were using the Blue Dragon Inn at Clarkson as a place to stay pending househunting in Toronto. Our family – my mother, father, young sister, Sophie, and myself – boarded there for the spring months. Father commuted by train to his office, where he was on the way to becoming general manager of the newly formed Canadian Press Cooperative News Service.

I was a timid, lonely child, somewhat at a loss because of the uprooting from Winnipeg where I had had one close friend, or chum, as we called her. Here in an Ontario village I knew no one, did not know how to make friends, and at the one-roomed country school the older children scared me. I buried my nose in my scribbler and tried to comprehend the arithmetic, "reduction" it was called – gallons to quarts to pints. Useless exercises, I thought.

And then, for two or three weekends, there you were! Tall, thin, boyishly built with silver-blonde short hair: a gamine, your fair and rosy skin contrasting with your brown eyes, soft as velvet and deep as a woodland stream. But what a tomboy you were! I had never met a girl like you, so rough, forcing me to wrestle with you as you seized hold of my arms. Only two years later, when we ended up in the same girls' school, did I discover the other side of your nature: sylphlike, darting through woodlands, leaping over streams, delighting to find rare wildflowers and birds. And reading poetry all the time, as I was.

When we settled in Toronto's Annex, I spent my first year at St. Mildred's School, run by Anglican sisters. Then my mother heard about Glen Mawr, a small boarding school on Spadina Avenue near Hoskin, where the principal, Miss Gertrude Stuart, emphasized the arts – music, painting, drama and the history of art. For the first term I was put into the fourth form, very timid with my classmates but determined to please my teachers and to "shine." As a result, after Christmas I was promoted to the lower fifth, where immediately I recognized you, Gina, the talkative tomboy who was always in hot water, always questioning. The teachers called you Eugenia, for you had been christened Myrtle Eugenia. How you hated that name! We suspected that the existence of the Empress Eugenie in your mother's day had something to do with that handle. To make up for it your classmates called you variously Gene, Jeanie, Jim or Gina. And you came to be, for us, the voice of resistance against authority.

Was it your wit that fascinated us, wit sometimes mingled with malice? I remember how, on a streetcar or sitting in the Owl Drugstore over a chocolate soda, you would make caustic remarks about people, not too softly. Or you would recount how "Every Monday morning I lean out from my window over the ravine and say hello to the garbagemen. They have the greatest way of talking back and joking. They make words exciting – honestly, Dee!"

One day, at school, we were looking out of the upstairs classroom window before the teacher came in when we noticed a man in the lane below, waving at us. Suddenly he unbuttoned his trousers and pulled out his "thing." "Don't look!" you warned loudly, pulling down the sash and drawing the blind. I think only the girls with brothers knew what was going on. The rest of us sat in stunned silence until the teacher entered the room. She must have wondered at the unusual quiet. "Eugenia, pull up the blind," she said.

Lesson hours at our private school were from nine o'clock to one, after which the day girls walked home to lunch. More often you had to stay on lunching at school, so as to take music lessons or play basketball. I was never good enough at these pursuits to be burdened by them. And actually, we both preferred to walk and talk, didn't we? We must have been an incongruous pair, you so tall and slim and I broader and shorter but with disproportionately long legs and arms. By the time we were in the upper fifth, we were very conscious of our bodies and uncomfortable with them. No matter how much the healthy and hearty gym teacher told us that menstruation was normal – "it proves you have entered into womanhood, not a time for misery" – we knew differently. Some girls suffered more than others and I was one of those. You were, as always, stoical.

During this period of late adolescence I was probably only aware of delight in your companionship. But you have tape-recorded what you experienced through participating in the Livesay household games. I remember how your own home life was strictly Victorian, with hours laid down for housework, study, shopping, piano practice, whereas my life must have seemed wildly bohemian. I love the way you have told it, with exaggerated gusto:

You see, the father and mother were so completely different. There was a constant pull for the two girls between them. And the father was, well he was quite a neurotic character, with a rather marked speech impediment. But a very brilliant man .... And the mother, while she wrote, it is true, I would think she was a very minor writer. The main thing about her was that she was extremely traditionally religious; she was a very staunch Anglican. Of course, Livesay's aim at home was to horrify her at every step. So every meal was a kind of bravado anti-religious thing on the part of Livesay with Mrs. L. kind of sighing and tearing her hair. Oh, and he used to do things like pasting up rather insulting but quite funny poetry on the walls about one or other of the family. Of course, she couldn't reply, this wasn't her means of defence. In fact she had no means of defence. As well as that, she was the most appalling housekeeper

– the house was mad. But the house had some lovely old English things, stuff Dee still has – old chests – still, it was a mad place, but full of books.

Well, I grew up there because it was so much pleasanter than my house. Livesay was terribly interested in the girls. His whole life centred on those two girls and their friends. And he used to treat us all like grown-ups and invite us to lunch at the Royal York and have green turtle soup and strawberries in December, and that sort of thing. When you're fourteen and you've been out to lunch with a real grown-up man, it is a tremendous thing. And they never really treated them as children really; they were part of the adult world.

As for boy-girl relationships, we didn't know any boys, did we? Except your elder brother. In any case, we wouldn't have known what to say to them; but we envied them their freedom (as we saw it) from the pains of growth.

What I remember is extreme nervousness in the presence of boys. However, we admired their firm, straight bodies and in order to look the same we strapped our budding breasts under tight cotton "brazeers." And I recollect my shock when you went so far as to wear only boys' striped cotton shorts instead of rayon panties. Of course we had to wear skirts, well below the knee; but we would have revelled in the blue-jean era! Whatever clothes you wore, Gina, you always looked striking. Perhaps you don't remember how, by the time we were in the sixth form and reading Michael Arlen's *The Green Hat* (read aloud to us, of all things, by our English teacher, Mary Jennison) you took on the role of femme fatale, wearing flared skirts, orange sweaters and, of course, a dashing green felt hat with a feather in it! At one point you even persuaded your parents to give you a white Russian wolfhound with which, on leash, you sauntered along Bloor Street between Markham and Spadina (such dizzying delights!).

Throughout these changing phases of yours I remained the sober plodding one. I was aware, of course, that I was dressed dowdily (my mother bought my clothes for me at Simpson's "on the bill"). But once when I had saved some pocket money I went downtown myself and bought a garment that fitted and suited my mood. It was of grey broadcloth, straight-lined, long-sleeved, high-necked – quite the uniform. At this time we were reading and acting out *The Merchant of Venice* in our English class, so you immediately dubbed my new costume "Dee's Jewish gaberdine."

Soon afterwards you led a movement to have the school adopt uniforms, as did other private schools such as Havergal or Bishop Strachan. This involved wearing a white tailored blouse, a short navy-blue serge tunic and long black stockings. My mother objected to the expense involved but my father, the Englishman, emerged from his usual detachment in such matters to state that I should conform to the school pattern. This solution left me free from worry about my clothes. My hair, however, was still long, drawn back with a barrette, whereas the other girls went along with the trend and were bobbed. But my hair was the only part of my physical being that afforded me any satisfaction. It was fine and wavy, nut brown in colour, with golden lights when I dried it in the sun. My eyes did not please me, being neither dark blue nor grey but something in between. In the summertime my face and arms were heavily freckled. Fine gold hairs had begun to show above my upper lip. So on a frosty winter day as we walked home up Spadina, you cried out in glee, "Dee, you should see yourself – you've got a white moustache!" You were often disposed to put me down in this way, and loudly; but I developed a defence – laughter. Rippling laughter surrounded us, wherever we went.

We both loved the woods and the Ontario countryside – that was the great bond between us. Whereas our schoolmates would spend their Saturday afternoons skating or "going to the show," which was, in those days, the stock company theatre, you and I would take the streetcar to the top of Yonge Street and go walking in Hog's Hollow, or saunter in the spring rain over the Rosedale Bridge. The trees waving below in the ravine seemed themselves to be weeping green rain. Then, after my father had built Woodlot, the first half of a house-to-be in the Clarkson woods, you would manage to get permission from your very strict parents to spend some weekends with me, especially in spring or fall. In your taped recollections of this period you speak of the two of us "sleeping in the woodshed." It was not properly such. My father had built, from rough-hewn logs, a woodshed beside the creek away from the main house, and he had added a room alongside big enough for two cots. We called this room "Cherokee." Through the windows at night we could see the white birches gleaming in the moonlight, hear the purling stream and the whippoorwill sending his loops of song into the silence. Wasn't it a fine place in which young girls could whisper their secrets?

Our first secrets concerned school: our classmates, our teachers and our poems, in which we vied with each other to astonish, amuse, delight. We even tried publishing a class newspaper, but after the second issue the principal announced, at morning prayers, that it was being confiscated and must never appear again. It had dared to make mild fun of some of the teachers' idiosyncrasies! You and I, however, after our first bursts of fury, were not really downhearted. We had discovered that our ruling passion was to write. My diary records that complication in these words:

Again, I am under the influence of Gina's brilliance. Her passionate need is to write, but she says that she cannot. *Compared with her I should be uncertain and depressed. But I am not .... Most people have a reason for living, that is to say, a philosophy, a creed. Mine is beauty. Gina, so coldly scientific, hasn't even that. There is nothing to balance her, to hold her. She should have been gifted in some definite way. It is terrible that she isn't.*

Nonetheless, you did participate with me, didn't you, in most of my literary exploration – the short stories, novels, plays, of Shaw, Chekhov, Ibsen. But it was the shared poetry that meant the most to us emotionally. We memorized some of Shakespeare's songs and sonnets, Robert Herrick, Andrew Marvell and the poetry of the Georgians: Walter de la Mare, Humbert Wolfe, Edward Thomas (my favourite). Then we discovered the women: Elinor Wylie, Katherine Mansfield, Emily Dickinson. This is how you recollected those experiences:

I am sure we were reading Emily Dickinson in School ... I can't really say why we liked, why I still like Emily Dickinson, and find her absolutely fascinating to read. It's just the small, the compact, the beautiful little structures ... And yes, of course Emily D. influenced Dee. Everything you read influences you. But it is quite obvious, isn't it, that in spots Dee is pure Emily Dickinson. Then, she doesn't stay within this little mould. I'm pretty sure we were reading Emily Dickinson long before going to university, because when we got to university, we were reading what were then contemporary writers, just eating up everything. Huxley and Virginia Woolf were at that point bringing out books. You got first editions. We'd passed through the historical period – all the ones who were dead; we'd read them all. Once I discovered Dee's family I spent all my time there, and read everything that they had, from Trollope on up because Livesay was very interested in anybody who read books and was interested in books and he just couldn't wait to press books upon you constantly. It was wonderful, it was like having your own private public library. And of course he discussed books with you, quite seriously. He would want to know your opinions. It is really rare when you are young that anyone wants to know your opinion, except to write it in an essay. It was a tremendous thing knowing that family.

Remembering all this, so vividly now after your words, I ask: is it any wonder we were called bluestockings? It is clear that though there were only two of us who were mavericks in that sixth-form class of a dozen girls, we formed a solid and indestructible minority – an "underground" if you like – in a small girls' school that had always been stamped with gentility.

Two of our teachers who played an important part in our development as free thinkers were Mary Jennison and Margaret Ford, our mathematics teacher. Both of them came not from "Toronto the good" but from the older, more mature culture of the Maritimes. In my last year in the sixth form (preparing for senior matriculation, grade 13) we had an ill-concealed "crush" on Margaret Ford. Young, dark, elegant, her mind was keen as mustard. No wonder we longed to know her better. The chance arrived when – of all things – Emma Goldman came to Toronto on a lecture tour.

As soon as my father heard about this event, he remembered how, as a young reporter in Winnipeg in 1908, he had been sent to cover Emma Goldman's lecture on Gorki. Her knowledge of Russian literature and her admiration for his heroes Ibsen and Shaw must now be communicated to the young things in his care – you and me. He himself took us to the first lecture, on Tolstoy, and thereafter we persuaded Margaret Ford to accompany us to others. Emma Goldman not only gave literary lectures, but she spoke as an anarchist and as an ardent feminist, advocating birth control. Our thirst for more led us to read Shaw's *The Intelligent Woman's Guide to Socialism and Capitalism* and the works of Marie Stopes, as well as *The Dance of Life* by Havelock Ellis.

Emma Goldman's stance had the solidity of a piece of sculpture; there was no fear in this woman. She took a stand. Everything about her was taking a stand. That was how Emma seemed to us, in spite of her thick guttural accent, which hindered easy listening. We were started on a direction completely the opposite from that of our fellow classmates.

Not for university were these girls of old Toronto families destined, but for "coming out" and going abroad and getting married. When Edward, Prince of Wales, visited Toronto, our senior graduating class was invited to the ball at Government House. Next day, there was great excitement when one of our lower-sixth classmates reported that her sister, Helen, had danced with the prince! You and I were not impressed (though doubtless we were envious). Ironically, our principal, Miss Stuart, whom we respected and feared, was not herself a society-oriented type at all but a graduate in Classics from Girton

College, Cambridge. She taught us scripture, with a choice of Greek or Latin. I chose Latin, and appreciated her teaching; yet I was easily subverted by you into seeing the principal as Enemy Number One. Remember that one morning we were expecting her to arrive at any moment to visit our seminar in "the alcove," a small attic corner where we would be carrying on with Caesar's *Gallic Wars*? We got to making puns, especially about the Roman manoeuvre of "attack on the rear." You searched the floor and produced a tack. "Let's put it on her chair!" you murmured, conspiringly. The half-dozen girls were amused, then stunned, as you placed the tack pointed end up on the principal's chair. "A tack on the rear!" With suppressed laughter but mounting apprehension we watched the time go by. Miss Stuart was often late for a lesson because of administrative crises in her office. We waited and waited. Finally her portly body appeared in the doorway and she marched to the small table around which we were sitting. "Now, what chapter were we at?"

"Attack on the rear," someone murmured.

"Well, let me see ..." Standing over the book Miss Stuart ruffled through the pages. "Oh yes, will you start translating, please, on page five." Our notebooks flew open, our eyes bent low. Would she or would she not ... sit down? Then, piercingly, the bell rang. End of lesson.

"Very well, then. That is your homework." And the principal sailed out of the alcove.

"Whew!" I was trembling with fear and relief. But you screamed with laughter.

It was escapades such as that one, though, that frequently did get you into trouble. Most serious was the punishment you received one noonday.

"If you think you are so important, Miss," the principal told you in front of us all, "I will ask you to be my guest today at lunch." And when all the boarders were seated in the dining room, the principal marched in, side by side with you, clothed in hat and gloves. You were ushered to the staff table and forced to eat with the teachers. Do you remember how you did not go home after lunch, as you were supposed to? Instead, you flew up the street to our house on Walmer Road. I was waiting for you, fearfully anxious. We sobbed and sobbed in each other's arms.

The next step for us acolytes was, of course, not to be writing to each other, but to be writing to the beloved. It was an accepted part of life in a girls' school – even in Toronto – that one developed crushes on older girls or young teachers. You and I were perhaps more overtly and ardently turned in that direction because we stimulated each other's emotions and fixations. I still remember the sense of the utter shattering of one's privacy, yet the exaltation derived therefrom, when we admitted to each other that we were in love with a fellow student. There had been others in the two previous school years and there were the two teachers who were wonderfully helpful in widening our knowledge of the world. But it was Julie, a new girl who came to Glen Mawr in our last, sixth year, who really aroused our awakening sexuality.

This was the year in which I had to study for honours matriculation, doing senior courses in English, French, Latin, German and modern history, as well as the horrors of algebra and geometry, for which both you and I had had to take remedial coaching. So the tension of looming examinations was ever with us. Perhaps even more powerfully with you, for you had decided – against your parents' advice of course – to take a pre-med course at the University of Toronto. And for this we well knew our polite ladies' finishing school had in no way prepared you. Science was not taught and we received generally poor mathematics instruction until the teachers Ford and Messervy came along during our two sixth-form years.

The way out of this tension was to indulge in an infatuation or crush. It was quite natural that the nearest object was a girl, perhaps a year older than we were, and very sophisticated. Julie belonged to one of Toronto's old families living in Rosedale. She told us that her parents had broken up, that she had had a mysterious illness, and that she had been sent to this boarding school for her finishing off before she would become a deb and enter the exclusive rounds of Toronto society. All this of course added to Julie's fascination, for never would *we* be admitted to such circles. Julie was patently headed for that sort of life. She was in no way a student intellectually inclined. She was swarthy, square-jawed, sombre: brown hair cut short like a boy's and with the most extraordinary dark eyes, "smouldering" in your phrase, the genuine femme fatale.

For once you agreed with me that we should keep our passion to ourselves and not flaunt it before any of our classmates. This might have reached Julie's ears and destroyed the sense of mystery she emanated. We wrote poems to Julie, but showed them only to each other. Things came to a climax, however, when the school year ended with its annual exercises, heavy with lilacs and the scent of make-up as the school play was performed. I was Lydia in Goldsmith's *She Stoops To Conquer*. Or was it Sheridan's *Rivals*? Parents came to the prize giving and the reading of marks. We were quite excited when my short story, "Siki," was awarded the prize presented by Katherine Hale, Mrs. John Garvin. But none of this mattered to us much, for we were scouring Bloor Street for flower shops. We had decided that Julie required one parting gift, one dozen yellow roses. We finally found this rarity, dispatching the offering with bated breath. On the card we printed a cryptic verse, but signed no names. Since we weren't boarders, we were unable to witness the opening of the gift. Then, suddenly, school was over.

We would have seen nothing more of Julie were it not for the fact that my parents were moving to our summer place in Clarkson and it was decided that I should stay in Toronto to prepare for the senior matriculation examinations. The principal agreed to taking me in as a boarder along with any other sixth-form girls who would be writing exams. Among them was Julie.

Was I right in thinking you were really envious of my opportunity to be so near the beloved? As time would reveal, the decision was most unfortunate for me, as I was the only serious crammer in the school and the other girls, including Julie, conspired together to keep me from studying. We had orgies of midnight feasts. I remember that after an unusually filling Sunday dinner in the school dining room, the girls went upstairs and immediately opened cans of tomato soup which they heated on their secret alcohol stove. The result was that the next day I failed to get a first-class in my modern history examination. I believe I only succeeded in English, French and Latin. Miss Stuart had drilled us so thoroughly in memorizing Horace, Virgil and Caesar that very likely we all sailed through that examination.

Once I was free of exams, you eventually managed to meet me to receive all the details that I had gleaned of Julie's life. But the intimacies of the boarding-school regime had somehow disillusioned me. Your pride must have smarted when I recounted, with insufferable superiority, the attitudes the girls had expressed during one jam session on marriage and babies. "Oh," Julie said, "have you ever seen a newborn baby?" None of us had. "Well, it's just a red blob. Not white, like us. Not *human*. The ugliest thing you can imagine." At that time I never consciously connected that description as being a confession. But *you* did! "So that was Julie's baby!" The mystery of the girl's illness was solved. But by now you had had experience as a counsellor at a children's welfare camp. You knew what was *really* happening in the world. I was to learn somewhat later.

That summer, when we were both getting prepared to attend university, marked the beginning of the end of our intense friendship. When I went to Trinity College, my courses, classmates and professors were so differently orientated from scientific ones at the pre-med level that we would only see each other perhaps on a Saturday afternoon, going for a walk in the ravine or sitting in your rooming-house digs listening to Beethoven's Fifth on your portable gramophone. Once a week at Convocation Hall there was an organ recital where we went together to listen to Bach, Haydn and Mozart. "You are like that music, Dee," you said once – your first praising, rather than mocking, words. I flushed; my heartbeat quickened.

By our second university year something else was happening to your emotional life that distressed me deeply. You were in love with a camp counsellor and had been on the verge of a lesbian relationship that summer. I hated to think of it. And now, on campus, you were going around with a known lesbian crowd. True, they were not regarded with the sense of taboo associated with "fairies" – our name for homosexuals. It was a peculiarity of woman's state that there were no laws prohibiting them from cohabiting. Perhaps this was because women did not pervert children, as it was believed men did? In any case, *The Well of Loneliness* was *the* book, yet it did not help me to accept your new role. This caused a rift. Then, the September of my third year, I went through my own rite of passage by leaving home for the first time and studying at Aix-Marseille from October to May. The possibility of travel was what had led me into taking modern languages in the first place. You, however, stayed home, struggling with medical courses. I received few letters from you. Then I heard from my sister at Christmas that you had had a breakdown, you had quit university and were sent to relatives in California to recuperate.

Not having your address, I wrote to my mother in Toronto, asking her to get it from your mother. In reply, she wrote:

We all felt a complete mental change was indicated, for her. Yes, dear, I do agree with you. The medical work is far too heavy to be undertaken, unless one had a body of (practically) cast iron. I never did feel it was the work for her, but the knowledge she already has will never come amiss.

Seemingly, on receipt of this letter I wrote you at once, probably in apprehension but seeking to assure you of my affection. Your reply must have thrown me considerably; but it is a moving example of your insight and resilience ever seeking a way out:

Feb. 28, 1930

I forbid you to delude yourself like this about me, just because you haven't seen me for a while. You must never, never call me "darling" nor think that I am necessary at all.

You know that, for me, living with you is the only real living, and always will be, but it isn't so with you. How you tempt me with Europe. You and Europe together would cause me to die of surfeit of ecstasy.

Really, though, I don't get any money when I am 21 so that, unless the family would consider it, it would be hopeless. As a matter of fact, they thought of you when they were about to send me away, but I refused to land on your doorstep and announce my presence calmly.

And then, funny things have been happening to me, so that you wouldn't like to be with me, and it might be dangerous. Since I left, I have no one, and am living quite secretly, and find myself constantly tormented like an adolescent boy, or a man about to enter a brothel. So that I am forced into religion, out of very preservation. Catholic churches are conveniently numerous here, so that in extremis I can rush into one. I keep seeing people, my sort of people, suddenly, anywhere, and wanting to begin to talk to them and have an affair. And it seems always that these people somehow know, and a very secret signal passes between us. Is there an underlying, hardly recognized sisterhood of these people?

You see, I am already a bit mad. Every time I go out I wonder, almost subconsciously, whether I shall somehow meet − anyone.

So you see, I am in a bad way, and, having confessed all to you, want not your revilement, but ... well, whatever else you have to give. How did you know that I'd left Meds, before I told you? Write me more, Dee.

Here is part of a letter from you, perhaps an earlier letter, written on campus at the University of Toronto:

Although such things are only ugly to you, the affair I had this summer will always remain very perfect and very beautiful. Unlike the business with V., it did not turn to ashes and disgust when I had a proper perspective upon it − on the contrary; it gained its true significance then. We were very perfect lovers, and always I shall keep last summer in my mind as one of the best and richest times I have ever had.

The following letter lovingly describes the women writers we shared:

March 11, 1930

I am reading Hedylus *[a prose book by H.D.], slowly sipping it as you advised. It's very lovely, isn't it – but a decadent sort of sophisticated beauty.*

Here is a picture of Gertrude Stein. Did you know she was thus? I wish you would dash up to Paris sometime and have a look at these people and find out just what G.S. is trying to do, and be the only one in captivity that knows and then tell me in words of one syllable and indelible ink.

Have you seen a picture of Elinor Wylie? She is strangely like Katherine (Mansfield) – dark and quiet. Here is the last poem in her posthumous book, Angels and Earthly Creatures – *do you not think it charming?*

Little Elegy

Withouten you
no rose can grow
no leaf be green
if never seen
your sweetest face
no bird have grace
or power to sing
or anything
be kind or fair
and you nowhere.

Recently I have dived into Amy Lowell. Such lovely free verse things alternating with awful rhymed hexameters (I think). There is one which begins "Hey my daffodil crowned, slim and without sandals"!

My next epistle to you must have been written to tell you about the experience I was having in the south of France, living *en pension* with a delightful family and becoming a close friend of Madame's daughter, Agnès. You replied:

Of course you realize that all my crushes were quite unphysical, up to perhaps Julie. And with C. there was and is no being in love, only that passion. Apparently such things are common in convents and girls' schools, and wise nuns recognize it and do what they can.

It was very nice of you to be strong and suppress it, Dee. But then you were always like that. How I love you. Will you read The Well of Loneliness *which presents the problem in an altogether different light? I'm not sure that scientists agree, but it's very well done – emotional energy quite extraordinary.*

Of course, the fact that you haven't a man this year accounts for this – but still can't you feel that all this is somehow useful?

It's become very necessary for me to see you and to get away from the family etc., for I've got to get organized into the universe … Wouldn't it be funny if I'd never met you. I would have been lost in the mire long since, I fear. You manage to illuminate things, you know.

By the time you got back to Toronto in April you had regained your self-confidence and optimism – linking up with the old college crowd and having "a rather jolly time." That was to be our direction in the future, for our fourth and final year as undergraduates.

April 7, 1930
My friend, your letters have arrived. I am home.

You were quite right, it was not difficult to discover that I was slightly neurotic as a result of seven weeks of repression. Your fears are groundless, however, so disperse them from your frigid couch. I am no longer suffering from a sense of sin or a sense of my own importance (same thing, according to Cabell) but have learned after divers buffeting to be, as you say, more unobtrusive. I also discovered in the course of my psychological reading, that I am not homosexual, but bi-sexual, a condition very common, apparently, among the Greeks – Plato and Socrates, etc. It was not then considered, and probably is not essentially abnormal at all, but has come to be considered so for reasons which would be interesting to find.

But be of good cheer, for I am, even to your discerning eye, in no way abnormal, and having a rather jolly time in the first rush of being home.

You know, it's awfully hard for me living alone. I'm not really asocial – quite the opposite, once my inferiority complex is overcome. So I continue to be scarcely ever alone.

By my fourth year we were friends again, but on a different level. You had left home and were living in rooms at the Old Elm on Harbord Street. This was a "tearoom" frequented by the students of Trinity College – the red-brick men's residence across the street. In this curious way you and I, Gina, moved for the first time with the same crowd. Literary and political discussions, Chianti parties, sleigh-riding on moonlit snowy nights when we sang to the jingling of the horses' bells – these were some of the delights. By now you had broken with your lesbian circle and were ready to take on the men. Alas for Dee! For as soon as there seemed to be a young man interested in me, the time came to introduce him to you. And there was no way I could be your rival. You were like a rocket among candles: lithe, sinuous, graceful. Your pale silver-gold hair worn longer than a bob, your brown eyes the colour of a river in sunlight, your rose-petal skin: how do I find the words to describe the young woman you had become? You were avid for love and sex and you thought of me as a sister in whom you could always confide. I think that you were simply not aware of how you were hurting me. I think that just to look at you, and then to hear you talk, the young intellectuals frequented the Old Elm. There were two young Englishmen constantly in that orbit: Frinkie (Frank Grimble) and his pal J. K. Thomas. There was Victor Lange, headed for an academic career. Most significant was the introduction I had, through my French professor, Felix Walter, to his friend, Otto van der Sprenkel. As I remember it, he had come from Holland to teach in the department of economics. A bearded, heavily spectacled man of the world, he held seminars on life in the Soviet Union, to which I was invited. After the sessions he would invite some of us to his apartment to listen to music, talk politics, play poker. Eventually, I brought you along to meet him, and while I browsed amongst his books (discovering T. S. Eliot for the first time), Otto entered into a sophisticated repartee with you. I knew what would happen: soon you were staying the night.

Although these "steals" pained me, they did not create a rift between us because by now we were having a lively social and intellectual life, of which we had been starved in our early university years. Otto, by introducing us to wide areas of knowledge about Marxism, socialism and communism, increased our thirst for travel. He was very convivial and open with students – unlike any professor we had met at the University of Toronto (except, perhaps E. K. Brown and Barker Fairley). Otto was a teddy-bearish and lovable sort of guy. But he was quicksilver. He did not really care, I think, who his woman was. And when you and he did go to Europe that summer he ended it by leaving you in Paris, alone. Do you remember how devastated you were? You cabled and telephoned from France frantically. "Dee, you have to come to Paris and help me!" I had been having a continual battle with my parents that summer because, with my sister, Sophie, I was running a coffee shop near campus in order to make money to get to the Sorbonne for a postgraduate year. Instead of waiting until October, I now wanted to go in August, to be with you. My father had already agreed to give me the Paris year if I would study for the *Diplôme d'études supérieures*, but he had been enraged by the coffee-shop project. It was my mother who persuaded him that I might have a nervous breakdown if I didn't go to my friend's support. She offered me the ship's fare, on the Cunard Line, from her own savings as a freelance writer; and so I went. And so, Gina, thus began another chapter of our loves and rivalries.

It is difficult for me to write about our reunion in Normandy. A journalist friend of my father's, Mrs. Josephine Hambleton, had recommended an auberge at Arromanches-les-Bains. We were to spend a week or more walking around the countryside, visiting museums, exploring the French way of life until such time as I would get myself enrolled at the Sorbonne in the department of comparative literature (where Professor Louis Cazamian held sway). But now we found it really hard to relate to each other. That summer, while you had been travelling through Germany and Spain as the mistress of Otto, the brilliant young professor, I had stayed in Toronto to run Charlotte's Coffee Shop. True, I had by now met up with a new group of friends – young newspaper people like Paddy Ryan, Isabelle Jordan, Nat Benson and Hugh. With Hugh I had my first affair. Though I was not in love with him, I felt a strong sense of empathy; but he was twenty-seven and ready to settle down. I certainly was not ready.

Otto's abandonment of you was cruel indeed. In your panic when you phoned from Paris you asked me for Tony's address there. You had already met this student friend of mine while staying with Otto in Barcelona. Alone in Paris you contacted him again and began exploring museums and art galleries through his perceptive eyes. Indeed, his exuberance and wit had been sufficient to rescue you from your depression, so that by the time I arrived in September you had put thoughts of Otto aside. You were still, however, in a very uncertain frame of mind, with moods fluctuating from despair to hilarity. I remember long walks through Normandy fields, fleeing from bulls; never really bridging the gap between our differing views on lifestyles. Actually, we became just plain bored with rural touristing and decided to get back to Paris. There we found the hotel where Tony was staying and spent a week or more living the café and boulevard life: three most innocent, though not virgin, Canadian students.

You and Tony seemed to be good friends – your wit made sparks fly at every meal. But between Tony and me there was a growing attraction that had begun back in Canada. One evening I felt ill and at my lowest ebb of hope for the future. I left the two of you and went to my room to break loose and have a sobbing fit. I knew I was in love.

You were concerned, Gina. You came to sit at my bedside. "What's the matter? What's the matter, Dee?" And I finally blurted it out: "It's just so crazy. Such a weird cycle. Hugh is in love with me and I am in love with Tony and he is in love with you and you are in love with Otto!"

"It's not true," you denied, vehemently. "It's perfectly obvious that Tony is crazy about *you*."

I didn't think you really believed it, but of course I wanted to believe it. Did you at that point decide on action on my behalf? Much later that night there was a rap on my door. It was Tony, in pyjamas and dressing gown. We caressed, passionately; but were still too shy to do other than lie down side by side and whisper our love.

Next morning I went to your room to share *le petit déjeuner* and found you in bed, raving feverishly. You had swallowed half a bottle of aspirin. I rushed up to Tony's room and somehow he, who spoke excellent French, found out by telephone how and what to give as an emetic. Trembling, we prepared a mustard drink and made you swallow it.

Oh Gina! From what depths of despair and loneliness did you do such a thing? Tony and I were now more close than ever before, working to save you. And yet – perhaps it was only a dramatic gesture on your part? Perhaps you had not swallowed all those aspirins? We were too distracted really to find out. In a day or so you had recovered and we took you to the Gare St Lazare to catch your train to Le Havre and the voyage home.

Tony, however, felt he could not bear to return to Toronto. He could do as I had done two years before, getting leave from the University of Toronto to take his third-year modern languages in Paris. That was how we came to set up housekeeping together on boulevard Saint-Germain, in a sixth-floor two-roomed flat. In between lovemaking and eating in cheap restaurants on the boul Mich (remember the automats?) we started in seriously to work at our *diplômes*, researching every day at the Bibliotèque nationale or the Ste-Geneviève ... a wonderfully happy and stimulating time, isolated though it was from friends and colleagues.

We looked forward to that Christmas, 1931, because you and Jinnie, another student journalist friend of mine, had decided to come to France for the holidays. That meant one week in Paris and twenty days at sea! How we were overjoyed to greet you on the station platform. "We're married!" I whispered. "Not *really?*" "No" – laughing – "not really." You have described my changed self with your usual acumen:

Like everyone else at this age, she had a tremendous thing going for someone at the university. He really couldn't see her for the trees. Being a poet, well maybe it wasn't worse for her than anyone else, certainly she could verbalize it, the whole agony of the situation. And she did ... Then later her sex life took a fine upswing and she had a wonderful year in Paris. This was really very satisfying and she blossomed, she just blossomed.

It is true that I blossomed but it was also true that my sexual needs were stronger than those of my partner. So the tensions grew if we were together too long – as on weekends. But we did begin to take a great interest in the French political scene. Tony was reading Marx and Engels and applying their theories to the current collapse of the capitalist system: unemployment, strikes and the buildup towards war, Hitler's goose-stepping youth. We read *L'Humanité* daily and began to go to rallies of the left where we witnessed police brutality against the organized and unemployed workers. On the five-mile parade commemorating the Paris Commune I heard for the first time the voices of young *blouses bleues* chanting their Brechtian slogans, songs and skits. Although I was writing love poems at the time (published years later as *The Garden of Love*) my social conscience was roused. I felt that a poem must speak more about the times. My first longer effort was entitled

"Père-Lachaise" (the name of the great Paris cemetery where the 1871 martyrs are buried). But in between these emotional "highs" we were both working doggedly at our Sorbonne theses.

Before the winter was over we decided to live separately again. Tony, I discovered, did not want an adoring, mothering love-mate. He thought I should learn to "stand on my own pins." I know he was right, but at the time I could not accept an independent feminist role. I was still in the romantic throes of the clinging-vine myth. Fortunately, perhaps, the demands of our research kept us parting and meeting that spring. I had to do a stint of research on the Sitwells at the British Museum, staying in London with a Livesay aunt. Daily Tony's letters came boating across the channel. But then he had to take off for Italy. By the time he returned to Paris I had moved into a modern flat at the Porte d'Orléans. It was rented by two sisters from Montreal, Andrée and Yvette Levy. The third sister, Simone, was living in student housing and studying art. When Tony returned from the south, he was not a little disconcerted by my new milieu, my growing independence and my socializing with friends of the Levys, mostly Canadian artists and graduate students like Leon Edel. However, for our last month in Paris, May to June 1932, Tony persuaded me to return to him. This time we found a suite far from the student world, on the east side, the working-class area of Ménimontant. At home, writing our theses, we saw no one but each other. For that short time it was blissful rather than claustrophobic. I had a scare about being pregnant, but happily the French birth-control system we had adopted, a small white cone inserted beforehand, had been effective. We were still deeply devoted when we set sail for Canada, bearing high marks from the Sorbonne (indeed, Professor Cazamian wanted me to stay on and do a *Doctorat d'état*). But at home in Canada, as you, Gina, were finding out, the Depression had struck and there were no more funds available from our parents for student travel. We had made it, just by the skin of our teeth!

That was a stormy summer, back living with my parents at Wood-lot, or staying alone part of the week in their Toronto house,

20 Rosemount, near St. Clair. Where were you that summer, Gina? I had not found you in Toronto. You must have been working at the children's welfare camp in Bolton. But by late August we all got together again, this time in an entirely new environment with a new set of goals. We became members of the Progressive Arts Club, meeting in an upstairs room near the Toronto Art Gallery at Grange Park. You, with Toby and Oscar Ryan, were in the theatre section; I was in the writers' group chaired by Ed Cecil-Smith, later of Mackenzie-Papineau Battalion fame. There I learned how to write agitprop for the magazine *Masses*. We were by now firmly attached to the party line and adamantly rebellious against our parents and their conservative views. So you and I decided to share a flat over a store at Charlotte and College streets, close to the university. You would be finishing a year in psychology and I was enrolled in Toronto's new School of Social Work. But before Christmas I had to face the fact that Tony had definitely broken off our relationship. You didn't put obstacles in my way, Gina, when in my misery I gave up living in our flat, and went back to my parents' house on Rosemount. I scarcely saw you any more and only my studies in social work and my new friendship with Maysie Roger saved me from doing more than just consider suicide. For I was still desperately trying to see and talk with Tony – only to discover that he was having an affair with you. I did not get over what seemed a terrible betrayal on both your parts until, in the autumn of 1933, I left Toronto and went with Maysie to Montreal to work in a Protestant family welfare bureau as an apprentice caseworker.

There we were thrust into the depths of the Depression under the most repressive regime in Canada. Montreal's unemployed were in daily confrontation with Taschereau and the laws of R. B. Bennett's Section 98. This experience was the most traumatic of my life up until then, but one I could no longer share with you. As far as I was concerned I was by then an active militant out on the picket line, writing and delivering leaflets, writing and reciting chants. That was the year when I was promoted from the Young Communist League to membership in the Communist Party, one of many like-minded young people who wanted to build the movement against war and fascism. The policy in 1934-35 was still that of a United Front of workers and progressives from the middle class. Being one of the latter I was chosen to contact organizations such as the YMCA, YMHA, church groups and welfare groups with a view to setting up a youth peace movement in Canada. When I returned to Toronto in June 1934, I met you again and we talked politics, without rancour.

By now you had married Lon Lawson, a man your own age with the same political beliefs. Together you were on your way to live for the winter in New York. Meanwhile, I spent the summer months engaged in the same activist directions as before, but with an added sort of experience as organizer-secretary for an office and shoe salesman's union. The Worker's Unity League slogan was "Organize the Unorganized." However unsuited I likely was for such work, I undertook it for the summer, having planned to go to New York in the fall and look for a job in social work. My plan worked. With my union card safely in my pocket, I landed in the great city by bus. Your apartment was in Chelsea, a few doors away from the offices of the *New Republic,* at that time a favourite journal of left-wing intellectuals. From the windows it was possible to see its much-admired literary editor, Malcolm Cowley, striding past on his way to work. There, you were studying acting and directing with Elia Kazan, Clifford Odets, John Garfield and other luminaries of the Group Theatre. This experience you used in helping to found the Theatre of Action on your return to Toronto in the fall and to direct its first production: Odets's *Waiting for Lefty.*

This was the last time, I think, that you and I, and now Lon, were in complete agreement about the role we had to play in combating fascism and the outbreak of war in Spain. In those days intellectuals were made to feel needed; we felt ourselves to be a part of a worldwide struggle.

Back in Toronto, much was going on in leftist circles. You were now something of an heiress, having reached the age when your grandfather's money could be released for your living expenses and for literary projects. With great zeal and enthusiasm for the United Front, you and Lon started a monthly magazine that was intended to rally middle-class intellectuals in Canada, as did the Left Book Club in England and *New Masses* in the United States. The result was a cooperative effort, *New Frontier*, a monthly journal to the left of the *Canadian Forum*, aimed at teachers, social workers, writers and artists. Even reading it today, we would have to admire its lively content of informed opinion. And you, Gina, were already a correspondent from Spain. You left Canada at this time to go with Dr. Bethune to Spain, where you drove an ambulance, at first for his blood transfusion unit and later for the Mackenzie-Papineau Battalion.

But in 1935-36, with Spain being murdered by Franco, working for that magazine gave me my first real opportunity to see myself in print, speaking out on the ills of the Depression. I travelled west, through Manitoba, Saskatchewan and Alberta to British Columbia, writing documentary reports about strikes, lockouts, demonstrations by the unemployed. All during those years I was in the main writing prose, documentary realism.

Well, as you know, I never returned east to live. As a government-employed social worker in Vancouver I married an unemployed Scot, Duncan Macnair, who had been helping me sell subscriptions to *New Frontier*. He was thirteen years older than I. Eventually he got a job and I lost mine.

Nineteen thirty-eight must have been the watershed of our youth. What we had worked for and dreamed it could lead into was a decade without war, without dictatorship, when man's urge for power and destruction might be curbed for good. Instead, the scene was dominated by Mussolini, Franco, Hitler and Stalin. You will remember, Gina, the tension of that year when all across Canada the forces of left and right were lining up, not for unity, but for power. Magazines like *New Frontier* folded, the United Front collapsed and in my seaport town, Vancouver, the Progressive Arts Club and the West End Community Centre, which we had built up in the old bathhouse at

Gina Watts Lawson, early 1940s

English Bay, were in disarray. This is not the place to reargue the validity of the party line, Chamberlain's appeasement of Hitler, whether we should vote "Peace" or take a stand, a war if necessary, to stop fascism. I remember well that in August and September 1939, you came out west on a speaking tour and stayed with Duncan and me on Pendrell Street, near Stanley Park. There were violent disagreements between us, but, now I cannot remember which sides we took! For when the phony war ended, when Stalin and Churchill formed their united front, when in Canada our friends and comrades were released from jail, we were all in favour of stopping Hitler.

Lon, who had become quite ill in the Don Jail, was released to join the army and you joined the Canadian Women's Army Corps. I stayed at home, with a son born in 1940 and a daughter in 1942. So our lines of communication were broken for many years, until, in the sixties, after Lon had emerged from university as a psychiatric social worker, you moved with your adopted children to Victoria, B.C.

Our lives crisscrossed, but never with the old intimacy. I admired the way with which you devoted your life to the Ban the Bomb antiwar campaign of the sixties and to supporting the Voice of Women movement. Yet it was ironic that your fighting spirit and aggressiveness hardened – all in the cause of peace! You were hard to live with, Gina, and hard on your own heart. You died too soon.

Today, it seems only fair that you, who knew me so intimately, who gave such impetus to my early poetry-making, should have the final word. Here it is, as told to Charlie Boylan:

You couldn't possibly compare Canada in the thirties with Canada in the sixties. This continent is untouched by any real kind of political conflict, just like it's untouched by any kind of war. We're innocents. Brecht was doing a political act. He was really involved in the Folk Theatre. If you are just writing poetry, you're not involved in this way. So I don't think Dee was terribly interested in political theory. I don't think she's got that kind of mind, that kind of interest. She was interested in people. And this is the thing about Africa: she wasn't terribly interested in the politics of Zambia or what kind of liberation movement was going on. It was how it affected the individuals that she knew. I think her interest is always a personal one. It has to be. You can't write poetry and have any other kind of interest. She is successful in her poetry mainly I guess because of the imagery. In most of her poetry she is not dealing with ideas, impersonal ideas, because she is not that kind of a poet. I don't remember it because there are ideas in it; I remember it because of the images.

And something of your old, stringent self, Gina, came out in these words:

I don't care if a person writes erotic poetry at a hundred. You don't read poetry thinking, "How old is the writer," do you? This is not the important thing. After all, if you had to look at Dylan Thomas's face while you were reading his poetry, it would take away a good deal because he is horribly homely. But this is not important.

And in this question-and-answer session with Charlie Boylan:

He: *Do you think [Dorothy Livesay] represents the woman's point of view?*
Gina: *For me that's a rather meaningless generalization. I don't know what the woman's point of view is.*
He: *Well, then, a woman's point of view.*
Gina: *Well, obviously she represents a woman's point of view!*
He: *Take the love poetry at the end of her last book, do you identify with it, understand it?*
Gina: *Yes, certainly. But can't men identify with it, too? I mean, is love poetry so divided between the sexes? Such things are only significant to women? I don't think so, but then of course I'm not a man.*

Not a man, my Gina. But with a toughness and intransigence that is still, in our age, attributed to the masculine. An uncompromising mind in a very sensitive and sensual frame.

So, Gina, in the thirties and forties you were the New Woman. Disagree as we did, your vibrant pace swung me along the same road.

The Writing Game

In Ottawa, my mother had been an enthusiastic ballroom dancer, so it must have been a disappointment to her that I was so awkward and self-conscious. We were taught how to waltz at Glen Mawr, using a chair as a partner, but I never learned how to dance, even though in those early teen years I was given extra, private dancing lessons. I could manage with a good teacher, but when faced with a young man, often as scared as myself, I was hopeless. A further disappointment, particularly for my father, was that I was so uncoordinated at gymnastics and games. JFB was a great tennis player and swimmer himself. He painstakingly arranged, when he built his tennis court at Woodlot, to have young men from the office come out and play foursomes. As I wrote in "The Ballad of Me," my astigmatism prevented me from seeing accurately. In addition, I had poor physical coordination, so my nickname became "Butterfingers." My only physical enjoyment was going for walks. Gina once persuaded me to go with her to the riding stables. They put me on a horse, but when I slid off – twice – and nearly got tramped on, that was the end of that.

So it doesn't seem strange now that when I could do something well – write – FRL and JFB seized on that with great satisfaction and pushed opportunities my way. After all, were they not writers? Failed writers, perhaps, but here was someone in their charge who might not fail.

Both FRL and JFB were self-educated, like many reporters, and they had no university degree. I think they were attracted to the newspaper game because they secretly longed to become writers. With the problem, however, of earning a living in the early 1900s and the equally difficult feat of getting books published, it was natural that their ambitions sought satisfaction in their children. As the first-born, very articulate child, I came in for the most attention. My father assumed responsibility for my education in reading, while my mother took on the encouragement of my writing.

By the time I was twelve, I had begun to find it a dizzying experience to write a verse and have it rhyme. But I did not want my mother to see it. Somehow the experience was my own, hidden in the back of my bureau drawer and not to be shared. However, one day when I was about thirteen, I came home from school to find FRL flourishing scraps of paper. "Why, Dorothy, these are real poems!"

I was enraged. "This is my room. My bureau drawer. How could you open it?" "Oh, I was just looking to see if you needed any clean handkerchiefs. Surely you don't mind knowing that these verses are good? And there are some places where I could show you how to do better. Look, the metre is wrong here." Thus she persuaded me to listen, then to let her send my verses to newspapers and magazines.

As luck would have it, my first published poem was in the Vancouver *Province*, which in those days had a high reputation as a literary newspaper. I liked seeing my verse in print, but was more thrilled when I received a cheque for two dollars. This I remember taking to school to show my friends, passing it on under the desk. "Dorothy! What's that note you are passing?" the mathematics teacher demanded. "N-nothing," I stammered. But she made me come up to the front and display what I had. It wasn't a note, but the cheque. My rating among classmates was high that day and I had got "the bug."

By the time I was sixteen, I had become ambitious enough to send out poems myself, to the *Canadian Magazine, Saturday Night,* the *Canadian Forum* and to the Canadian Authors' Association. It must be said on FRL's behalf that she did not change the sense or the imagery of my poems, she only sought to emphasize the requirements of metre and the delights of repetitive verse forms. She herself loved Robert Herrick's poetry and the French forms: rondeau, rondel and triolet. I tried them out to please her, but I was not good at them. Instead, since Mother subscribed to *Poetry: Chicago* (which had published her poems and her Ukrainian translations), I became more interested in free verse and the imagist movement. I remember being particularly attracted to Richard Aldington, H.D., Ezra Pound and Amy Lowell's renditions from the Chinese. As well, FRL bought most books and anthologies of Canadian poetry that appeared in those boom years of Canadian nationalism, the 1920s, so I knew and admired the free verse of the first Canadian imagists, Arthur Stringer and Louise Morey Bowman. Bliss Carmen's Sappho poems attracted me much more than his sentimental rhyming lyrics, but the latter were the only ones put into school readers.

What kept me humming was writing that my mother never saw, jealously guarded in scribblers at school and shown only to Gina – satirical sketches of classmates and teachers with apostrophes to our latest crushes. I was no longer lonely. I had an audience, a kindred spirit, to use L. M. Montgomery's revered phrase: Gina, the beautiful, wild tomboy, who led me down paths my mother knew nothing about. The one creative idea we did share was with my father: our mimeographed magazine, "Fortnightly Frolics of the Lower Fifth." JFB provided the paper and the typing, done by a junior office boy. This rather nonliterary venture only lasted two issues as it was banned, after all, by our principal.

Gina's special influence on my writing came from her passionate interest in poetry. In literature class we had had as a text Professor Alexander's *Shorter Poems* and our great delight came from reading the seventeenth-century lyric poets. I still remember vividly one epiphany we shared, on discovering the lines, "O let me sleep embracing clouds in vain / And never wake to know the world's disdain," by Dryden. A shiver shook us, hearing the sound of those long *ay* vowels, sifted through with the *ee* sounding vowels. Although we were equally interested in short stories, novels and plays – Shaw, Chekhov, Ibsen, all my father's favourites – and were ambitious to write prose, it was the shared poetry that meant the most to us emotionally.

Gina not only possessed an intense delight in poetry, she was also well trained in music. When we reached university, though registered in different colleges, Gina invited me to her attic digs to listen to her record player. Gina's knowledge of music made me realize my own inadequacies as a listener. Because of this, I took an evening course in Dalcroze eurythmics, taught by Madame Madeleine Lassere, and I believe this kinesthetic activity strengthened my feeling for rhythm in poetry. But it did not change my stiff, uncoordinated body movements. I remained too self-conscious to let go and dance. Instead, the words did that.

All my knowledge of love came from books. In this sense my father had not failed me. Indeed, he was probably the only parent in the city of Toronto in the twenties who combined a passion for Henry James with a passion for women novelists: Jane Austen, Charlotte Brontë rather than Emily), Virginia Woolf and Katherine Mansfield. It was a somewhat precious, specialized reading. The social frustrations women faced in the nineteenth century were no less galling than the social freedoms of the twentieth; in neither case could a woman be wholly a human being. For an Englishman, my father was unusually sensitive to this problem. Perhaps it was because of his gentle mother, artist aunt and artist sister that he looked upon gifted women in the same way that a Frenchman does: not as rivals to be secretly resented, but as phenomena to be appreciated. In this, I understand now, JFB was typically neither British nor North American.

Charlotte Brontë's life filled me with the greatest curiosity. The isolated world surrounded by illness and death parallelled her passionate desire to live, to love and to be loved. What she underwent at the hands of the Belgian schoolmaster who was not great enough to give in return; or at the hands of her father, so adamant against her marriage to anyone; and, finally, in her fortieth year, as wife for a few months: all this pain burdened and yet enriched the novels: they set me on fire.

Yet, to tell the truth, it was not reading others' books that drove me to write poetry. It was the world of nature, the sun and the seasons, the Clarkson woods and Toronto's elm-lined streets and gardens. Perhaps because I was born an autumnal child there are many notations in my diaries describing the dying season:

Clouds so faintly outlined that they are scarcely seen, move perpetually across the pale sun, across the pale sky. Wind, rising and falling, blows down a few stray leaves from the maples, from the poplars. There is a breath in the air. Haze creeps up from the woods.

In October, I remember:
   Autumn's flames
   Burn out the cool green pools
     of summer shade

Throughout these teen years, music also was a strong influence. At age fourteen I was writing:

Poetry and Music are one, for Poetry is Music. There is rhythm, there is passion in music; there is Love and there is Hate. I love prose – it seems akin to God. At times I long to spend my life making prose ... But alas! There is music in my soul as well. Nothing will daunt my music; it swells and swells, sometimes leaving me glad – more often, leaving me sad. I wish the music would go away and let me have prose – and yet – I love my music.

I remember as an unalloyed pleasure our evening meal. Supper, we called it. After JFB had come home from the office and had his nap, the maid would ring a little brass bell and we would sit down to a meal of roast, steak or chops, always with two vegetables besides potatoes, to be followed by lemon, rhubarb or apple pie, rice pudding, lemon cake pudding or floating island. Throughout the meal, whether we had guests or not, JFB would discourse on the political and literary events of the day. So certainly in my younger teens it was not a time for family squabbles or personal anecdotes; it was a time for listening and sometimes venturing an opinion.

My memory reveals different dinner scenes (we never called it "supper" when guests came; we called it "dinner" and the maid wore her black uniform). Once Charles G. D. Roberts was invited to dinner at which we were to have JFB's favourite entree, roast lamb with mint sauce. To begin with, there were no drinks. We never had liquor, wine or beer in the house unless JFB had fallen off the water wagon. Consequently, there was no before-dinner drink for the great poet, who had given a recital in Toronto. Then, when the immigrant girl brought on the roast and JFB began carving it, he found it was rare – and lamb by English standards had to be thoroughly cooked to a warm brown, unlike roast beef. Major Roberts obviously agreed. The meal was not enjoyed. My father seemed ill at ease, avoiding the subject of the war. I knew he considered Charles G. D. Roberts a fake because, though he had been made a major in England, he was never in the line of battle.

After dinner, JFB disappeared into his upstairs library and my mother sought to please the poet by playing some Beethoven sonatas. She played with feeling, but with no technique. The poet urged me to play a Chopin prelude which FRL had told him I knew, but I stubbornly refused. I knew that I had no technique either. Instead, we discussed poetry, the modern free-verse movement. "The hardest poetry to write is free verse," Roberts told me. I didn't disagree; that would have been to admit to being a mere dilettante, which I did not believe I was. For me, though, free verse was the easiest to write: the rhythms, so close to speech, delighted me. But I did not think there was much of a science to it. If only Roberts had told me about his youthful poetic games with Bliss Carman and Richard Hovey at his home in Nova Scotia I might have warmed to him. If only he had told me about his editorial days on the *Week*, a Toronto literary magazine of the 1890s. Instead I was sharply aware of his worldliness, his elegance. I dared to challenge this: I called him the grandfather of Canadian poetry, and this miffed him.

By the time I was at university my mother had begun collecting recent Canadian poems for an anthology that was never published. During my freshman year, rather awkwardly, I would be introduced, usually at tea, to some young caller who had brought his poems for FRL to see. Fascinating and debonair was Robert Finch, but much too formal and British for my tastes, whereas Raymond Knister drew me close because of his infirmity, a severe stutter. Patiently I listened as he told me about the imagist poets he had met in Chicago and Iowa: Carl Sandburg, Amy Lowell and the great editor herself, Harriet Monroe. Also at that time I attended poetry readings by the Irishman "AE" and by E. J. Pratt.

After one such gathering a strange, snakelike young man asked if he could call. He was the composer Caesar Finn. I was dubious but also curious. With unusual tact, my mother withdrew from the scene, leaving me to entertain this man by the fireside. I was like a flower, he said, in a glass case: it was time that I burst the bonds. But within myself I knew it wasn't time, and I told him so. He never came again.

At university, my longest, most ambitious poem was written in iambic pentameter: "City Wife." During the raw Toronto winters I hated the city streets, the serried ranks of red duplexes. I longed for spring, for then we would begin spending weekends at Clarkson, where I was free to roam the woodlands and farms. The farmer's life had fascinated me since I had spent a week during the Winnipeg strike on our housegirl's father's farm. Although the farmer was free from city fret, I saw that he was chained to his chores, as was the farm wife. In agreement with Raymond Knister, whom I got to know through his visits to my mother, I felt that the farmer, although part of the rhythm of the natural world, was insensitive to its beauty. Above all, he was insensitive to the personal needs of his womenfolk, their very psyche. Like Knister, I was reading Martha Ostenso's *Wild Geese* and Grove's *Settlers of the Marsh,* both books banned from western libraries.

Of Grove's work, I particularly loved his essays in *Turn of the Year,* which unhappily has never been republished. So, walking along woodland paths, skirting the fields so free of snow and awaiting the plough, I conceived a story about a city girl who married a farmer. It turned out to be not a short story, not prose, but a lyrical outpouring which, in my second year at university, won the Jardine Memorial Prize of $100.

It was after that award that I became known on campus as a bluestocking, which lost me a social life, but which eventually led me into the literary circles around the *Varsity* and the University College Players' Club. At the time, the possible role of women as writers was being very much questioned. Men had their literary and student organizations; women had theirs. But in drama, women were much in demand. Though I had no main role in the plays I tried out for at Trinity College (I had wanted to be Aase in *Peer Gynt* and Masha in *Three Sisters*) eventually I was given a character role as the old mother in Lady Gregory's play *The Dragon.* It was fun learning the Irish accent. From that time onward I identified with old women. Sylva Gelber, however, saw me as an Eve for a workshop production of the prologue and first act of *Man and Superman.* Paul Gardener was Adam and under Sylva's direction we did a very stylized dialogue. The only trouble was that the serpent was supposed to be cunningly concealed on stage behind some bushes. When I reached out to stroke its head, the audience burst out laughing. There was no serpent visible. Such forays into drama were a release for my pent-up emotions.

I was asked to put on a play at St. James Cathedral for a young people's drama group and managed to produce with them scenes from *Little Women.* Although I knew nothing about directing, this adventure led to my being invited to the Chautauqua summer drama and poetry session to help a cousin of mine, Margot Gordon, direct plays. It was there in that summer cottage atmosphere of the Muskokas that I met again some of the travelling poets: E. J. Pratt, Charles G. D. Roberts, Wilson MacDonald and the University College poet and editor Nat Benson. Benson was a protégé of Roberts's and, as I remember, wrote long Greco-Roman dramatic poems in blank verse that I thought were appalling. I was also disgusted by the poetic pose that dictated there must be a young adoring maiden constantly visible at the poet's feet. (Where she lay in private was an element not mentioned!) Nat had Margot direct one of his dramatic poems, with a young student as leading lady. Unfortunately, she could not act. The summer holiday audience must have been baffled if not bored.

Luckily for me there were on campus young men not seeking to put women in a stereotyped role. With these I felt happy and at ease. Nonetheless, university life was galling.

During my first and second university years, my parents took it upon themselves to get my poetry published. Through Mazo de la Roche, who had won the *Atlantic Monthly* Novel Award in 1927, FRL knew the editor of Macmillan, Hugh Eayrs, an Englishman who took a keen interest in the Canadian literary scene. FRL worked with me in selecting poems for a chapbook. This was the collection called *Green Pitcher*, published in 1928. Some of the poems in it were the sort that I wrote for and shared with Gina. Others sprang from my walks in the farm woods. "Impuissance" won a prize in a Montreal authors' competition. The origin of that poem was a drive with my father along the old highway beside the St. Lawrence. It was a moment of deep summer, July or August. We stopped for a picnic beside a field where haying was in progress. The image of the boy on his hay cart was so vivid I wove my emotions around it. "Fantasy in May" came from a most joyful spring moment in Toronto. At a little park on Walmer Road, a bed of tulips was blowing in a mad spring wind; I called them "harlots." The literary reaction to this poem, and this book, was hard to believe. Using the word "harlots" was considered to be risqué.

This was a time in my youth when I hoped for love and understanding, but instead was encouraged to seek public acclaim. Secretly, I poured out my feelings in my diary and poems. Those poems were such personal expressions it seems strange now to think that they were made public! I did not will it, but I went along with it. What I did not know at the time was the extent to which JFB was pushing the book with his newspaper friends and requesting reviews. Years later, after his death, a telltale file came to light. It is little wonder that, though I was so much an innocent abroad, I must have been feeling, in my unconscious, that I was being made an object to appease my parents' frustrations. I must have been wondering, for I felt there was a certain hostility emanating from newspaper editors. "Father's pet" was the last thing I wanted to be. So as soon as I could I asserted my own independence of thought and expression.

From the lyric period of my youth, undoubtedly my best, most finished poems were in *Signpost*, my second book, published in 1932. These poems came from the intensity of unrequited love; it was an infatuation rather than a realistic affair. It is evident from his correspondence that my father pushed for the publication of this book, also. *Signpost* did not appear, however, until I was away from Canada for a second time in France.

E. J. Pratt was probably the Canadian poet I most admired when I was a fledgling. At Victoria College, University of Toronto, he had been given a teaching position in the English Department, under Professor Pelham Edgar. The congenial atmosphere in the late 1920s must have afforded him more leisure time for writing, no longer in the style of his first book, *Newfoundland Poems*, but in mock-epic style. I remember that my mother took me to an evening reading of his "Witches' Brew," the humour of which he enjoyed as much as did his audience. I saw him as a small, energetic, balding man, with something elfish in his demeanour.

When I met him again in the Muskokas, Pratt spent an evening on our cottage verandah, with a full moon fluttering its way across the lake. He regaled the young people, boisterously describing his exploits as a student itinerant preacher and Bible salesman. As his wife later commented to me: "After doing a sermon, he never had the heart to sell a Bible to the people who put him up." He seemed a happy, genial man, but there were stories of his irascibility. He could not abide "side" or pretension in people and could be very rude if he disliked someone. He found both Wilson MacDonald's and Frederick Philip Grove's arrogance quite irksome and resented their lack of gratitude for hospitality rendered.

From my early student days I was conscious of the rivalry between Pratt and Roberts. Roberts had had all the accolades, as the unofficial poet laureate, and it seemed as if Pratt had the ambition to replace him. Certainly I caught a glimmering of Roberts's sense of injustice when I did research on Pratt's "The Cachelot," for Roberts had written and published his beautiful long free-verse poem "The Iceberg" several years earlier. Perhaps this was my first experience with plagiarism.

My first contact with Wilson MacDonald was at Glen Mawr. Wilson was doing a tour of Canada, I think, covering just private schools. It appears he earned his living that way, but I don't imagine he received much of a fee. The entire school of girls was assembled in two classrooms with folding doors which opened up to make an assembly room. Usually term-end piano recitals were held here, but this morning was something much less boring to look forward to; a very dark-haired, very black-eyed slender figure came before us. It seems to me he wore a black suit that emphasized his clerical appearance, and then he opened his book *Out of the Wilderness* reverently, as if it were a Bible, and began in a high singsong voice to deliver his poems. Some of them we liked – the music and rhythm were appealing – but when he came to a very coy poem about a little girl we were nearly suffocated with suppressed laughter. For the title of the poem was "Little Brown Dee" – my nickname was Dee! He rhymed this line with "To whit to whee"!

In the literary world there was much (sometimes malicious) gossip about Wilson's peculiarities. In those days anyone who refused to eat meat and lived on raisins and nuts was considered to be a real eccentric. I was shocked when, while professing to be a vegetarian, Wilson criticized one charming Halifax hostess as being "the worst cook in Canada."

But Wilson also had another trick up his sleeve, one that revealed the demonic side to his character. He was a magician, and performed at boys' schools and at university gatherings. One such was held at my cousin's apartment, to which I was invited. There were about twenty fourth-year students sitting on chairs and on the floor whilst Wilson stood in the middle and did disappearing tricks with a ring and a scarf. Quite a discussion arose as to whether this involved hypnotism. "Oh, no! But I *can* hypnotize – if any of you would like to try!" No one did, or not that I remember. Then I asked the question: "Does your hypnotism extend outside this room, to a psyche not present in the flesh?" "If I know them," he answered. As the party broke up, he drew me aside and said, very low, "Two A.M."

I went home in a state of excitement, for a very good-looking student ahead of me, whom I had always wanted to meet, was present at the party – as was his fiancée. Stephen was therefore out of my ken, and yet I was infatuated. I must have got to bed before midnight because I heard the clock chiming downstairs from the fireplace mantel. But sleep did not come. I tossed and turned. One A.M. chimed. Finally it seemed I was about to drop off when "One-ne-ne Two-oo-oo," the clock chimed. Immediately I was enveloped by the presence of Wilson. Indeed, he invaded my very bed. "What do you desire?" he seemed to be saying, like a wizard in a fairy tale, and all I could whisper, but with my whole body, was "Stephen. Stephen. Stephen!" Then Stephen's aura came before me, Wilson's gradually vanishing.

I was startled beyond belief. I could of course have called out to my parents, but no such thought came into my head. It was my body that was possessed. The next day I could not rest until I had told it all to Gina. Her response was to tell me that the anaesthetic effect was not Wilson's doing, but my own. It may well have been. My diary records:

What I wished shows that my subconscious was working, and was susceptible to any mental influence. A queer business at all events. But in saying that, I feel no egoistic satisfaction. There is no fear of my being stupidly obsessed by it: I can still regard "ego" as amusing and dangerous.

My first two years at university were both interesting and depressing. I determined to make use of the university's offer to modern-language students to spend the third year abroad. Having done well in my second-year examinations, I applied for permission to attend the university at Aix-Marseille. My father had agreed to give me a monthly allowance. What excitement when I was accepted!

Rites of Passage

One: Aix-en-Provence

It seems to me now that my eight months in Provence, from September 1929 to May 1930, were more rewarding for my creative development and self-knowledge than any previous time. I was existing on three fronts: learning how to break with the family and be on my own, absorbing and evaluating manners and ideas outside my Canadian experience; clarifying my views on being a woman and finding some challenging ideas through my reading and through my friendship with a girl my own age; and being obliged to face the future – how to earn a living? This last kept me in constant dialogue by mail with my father. Our differing views and choices were revealed first in letters, but they led up to the confrontation with my father in person, in his native England. There my first outright defiance of parental authority took place.

When I first broke away from my family I was at the end of my eighteenth year, but my leaving home for the south of France was really only like being a puppy on a leash. My father met all my financial needs, so in return I wrote weekly letters either to him or to my mother or sister, Sophie. As well, I kept a diary that recorded life *en pension* in Aix-en-Provence.

It was to be an experience for which I have been ever grateful to my parents. I was still, at nineteen, very much their cushioned child; and

D.L. at age nineteen before sailing for Aix-en-Provence

though there had been flare-ups of rebellion, as my diaries and letters reveal, I depended emotionally on my home relationships and support. Two elements created my excitement. First, I would be free of lectures, essays, examination – the grind that was becoming such a burden. Second, I knew that although I would be attending classes in French and Italian at the University of Aix-Marseille, I would nonetheless have more time than I had had in Toronto to do some sustained writing, particularly in prose.

It was not a year for writing poetry. That direction seemed to have finished with the end of my second year at university and the end of my unrequited love for a senior student. Now, aside from my French studies, I was deeply absorbed in the prose of Katherine Mansfield and D. H. Lawrence. My goal was to become a novelist. In this my father encouraged me. "Put it all down," he seemed to be saying.

And I did, in a letter written early in 1930:

This seems like a good moment for a letter. It is raining, so I cannot hang my weekly washing out of the window to shock the neighbours. My room smells rather soapy, in spite of the narcissus, jasmine, violets and yes! periwinkles sitting about on table and dresser. Agnès and I found them the other day on somebody else's property; and I remembered at once the Benares wood carpeted with the blue flower and the pale white and green lily-of-the-valley.

I would indeed like to feel as romantic as you do about Canada. I think I do as far as the country itself is concerned. But the way of life is American. If people ask me here what differences I see between Europe and Canada they are always American differences. The virtue of Canadians now, as you say, and their great distinction from Americans, is their poverty. But that cannot last. The country is too rich in natural resources. You speak of a "hardy, northern people" forgetting that we are not Icelanders with only barren rock and winter for our sustenance. As I see it, a natural and geographic law binds us to the States, not to mention the bond of a mixed, transplanted race. We will be different as the Middle Westerner is different from the Virginian, as Quebec is different from Ontario. Our individuality will remain, but our spirit is that same raw, uncultured yearning for greatness that grows to the south; and we will learn by the same years and the same blows, I believe, what Europe knows: that greatness is not physical.

So, for the sake of its landscape, for the sake of its youth, Canada is the place to live in. But it is too wide, with too many differences in each province, to be a whole, except as a part of the natural whole of North America. Patriotism is a very narrow thing: it is not France the man of the south loves, but Provence. The aim of the politician is to glorify localism. What he is really trying to do is to make Provence tolerant towards Normandy (Quebec towards Ontario) and thus establish a sort of chain of compromise which looked at from afar seems one of identity.

That identity is (politically) necessary. I admit that. But spiritually it is of small importance. A poet, for instance, impregnated with the abstract idea of "Canada" would be a bore and a failure. But impregnated with Halifax and the sea; or Quebec and the habitant; or Virginia and the Negro — there you have the spirit that will count! England is fortunate in being small; England is great because her localism remained undisturbed and was synonymous with spiritual identity.

So art in Ontario will be a different flower from art in Quebec.

Four pages of theory when I had meant to write a personal letter — feeling very much in the dumps about my future. Sophie, now that she is taking root, will grow straight upward. Her creative energy is in herself. But writing is a more hazardous game, and my will is always in danger. I could very easily stop you know, and never write a line, if I had some very absorbing job — such as yours. As a kid, in games, I was always the leader, but later on poetry rather chased away what must have been a certain executive ability. If I had a magazine to boss, you know, I would be fearfully busy and utterly happy: because one half of me is constructive, observant and critical. I could stifle the other.

Indeed, I was in doubt about my writing life, as this letter to Gina reveals:

It's queer how a book one reads so often is a frame to one's mood. More than that; more than reading what you have a mind to read. Finding, rather, by chance, words marching across a page that have marched, half veiled, through your own thought.

On the boat Bill Wallace said: "You say that only the real artist can define art. How then can you and I define poetry? We are not real poets."

It shocked me. I had thought I was more than Nat or Harry, more than the little people. But it isn't true. It's just being young, as all the other forgotten artists were young, and topped the world. Because a certain fire blew through me and has passed now. I always defined creation as something coming from without – that is how youth feels it. But creation is rather a fountain within, a dayspring that will not fail.

How can it be that just stepping on this foreign soil, talking to no one, convinces me overwhelmingly that I am nothing? What is it? I am remote from books, pictures, music ... What is it? And do not laugh. It is so. I cannot write: there is no power in me. I feel ordinary – and do not regret it. I thought, before, if I could not write, life was useless. I do not feel it now. Life is here, here; and solely living it is enough.

Do not call it treachery, fear, weakness. I tell you there is no flame within me. Yet I am not grieving ... I don't suppose seeing things as they are is a time for grieving.

The glory has departed: and I am as one of these, contentedly. Yet is there any man, is there even Chekhov, who has said and said again how extraordinary life is. If I could only give the curious flavour of it to some one ... to someone. For it must be saved, it must be cherished, it must never be forgotten.

Here it is, all the taste of it in my mouth, the light of it in my eyes – and I am helpless. I cannot deliver it.

So I suppose I will go on, peering around the cloaks of the artists to see if they are doing the job rightly, as I see fit.

But the words marching on the page. Yes.

"Mais nous ne sommes pas des poêtes, mon cher Bouldreys, nous sommes des reveurs, c'est-a-dire des paresseux."

Every day in the new old world was fascinating. That first pension where I stayed from September to February, getting acquainted with the French manner of life, receiving very poor nourishment (as I think of those meals now), led me to absorb some of the literature of eighteenth-century France: the letters of Mme de Sévigné, *Emile*, the journals of Jean-Jacques Rousseau and the fiction of Alphonse Daudet. By great good fortune the Villa Ensoleillada was a new bungalow-type house tucked into a larger property called Clos Cangina. From the university I had obtained the address of Mme Chaumery, who owned the largest house in the Clos, La Terrace. I called there to find out if there was a pension close by, or if she herself took students in. The door was opened by a heavy-set, dark-haired girl about my own age, who was as startled as I was to hear my stumbling French. But she was warm! She welcomed me in with such heartiness that I felt at home at once. And sitting in the elegant salon, talking to the old cronelike grandmother, Mme Chaumery, I managed to make my plight known. I was a Canadian student searching bed and board for the university year. Agnès de Lombardon, for that was the young girl's name, decided to lead me across the way to the pension of Mme Julien. She was quite a beautiful young widow with three children, who had spent most of her life in Cochin-Chine. It was soon apparent that she despised the native people, *les annamites*. She had a charming manner that covered a will of iron and a flaring temper. But for lack of any other clues, I decided to take the small room offered. The previous year it had been occupied by two Scottish girls, so there were continual references to the doings of *"les ecossaises"* and to the speed with which they had learned to speak French.

Because the widow's house was next door to Agnès's grandmother's villa, I was enabled to develop that friendship which was one of the happiest of my life. Was this because of the distance from my home or because we so rarely saw each other, after the one very intimate year? Or else because she was a truly beautiful character – saint, if you will – and so a person whom everyone must love? I wrote about her in the story "The Glass House" and in a poem, "The Voyage Out."

Agnès de Lombardon was aged seventeen to my nineteen but she was bigger and heftier. Without knowing a word of English, she was able to understand my stumbling French and to laugh uproariously at my mistakes as we tramped over the hills of olive and grape orchards or climbed into the pine forest behind her mother's house, La Havane. She was a romantic, a child of nature, with none of the glamourous characteristics I had imagined were a part of being *une femme française*. Her sallow broad face was enlivened by warm dark eyes, laughter and mimicry. She was passionately fond of the outdoor life, of labour in the fields, of the care of animals and, as well, she possessed a wide knowledge of all the flora and fauna of that Provençal landscape.

She lived with her widowed mother and two brothers *à la campagne* at Tholonet, on what is now the route de Cézanne. Indeed, her mother's house, La Havane, was almost next door to the Chateau Noir, where Cézanne had lived. And although Aix itself had ignored its native son, the de Lombardon family and Agnès's aunt in particular, an amateur painter, delighted in his painting and the way he had revealed their beloved countryside. It was this countryside with its view of Cézanne's Mont Ste Victoire that fascinated me, infected by Agnès's passion for it. She loved to climb the hills, to hike to the Barrage Zola, where she introduced me to the pine trees, the mossy forest, the foliage, the rocks, the view. For the first month I understood hardly a word of her impassioned talk. But it was clear I was acting as a release for her feelings, her sense of rebellion against severe family constraints.

Here is a diary notation from November 10, 1929:

Agnès and I walking beside the little stream. The sun had gone out, but the tapering poplars shook their yellow leaves like candle flame. "Now if I could only have a tree like that in my room!" So immediately she clambered up, rough and eager as a young animal, and tore off the branches ruthlessly. "Pour votre chambre. Oui. Vraiment! Pour votre chambre." Afterwards we found bright crimson berries, plump and square as pin cushions. "Ah, ah, ah!" she seized them in her arms. "Maintenant, pour vous!"

Agnès scarcely knew her father. He had been killed in World War I. He had married for love, running off with a vivacious young woman of Aix who had no claim to be of the aristocracy, but who was well educated, well bred, if not financially well endowed. Her husband's mother, who claimed to be Comtesse de Lombardon, a title of recent nineteenth-century origin, was so snobbish that she never forgave her son for marrying beneath his rank. Lise bore him two sons and, before he was killed, a daughter, Agnès, in 1911. The sons came first and every sacrifice was made to cater to their wishes and their education. As I saw them, neither one was worth the effort. They were egocentric, spoiled and inveterate womanizers. Agnès was just the baby sister, sent to convent to be finished off, and then brought back home to find a husband. A young farmer was thought to be suitable, but Agnès utterly rejected the idea.

Thus it was understandable that the widowed mother and grandmother, abandoning all hope of seeing Agnès settle down to domesticity, marriage and children, had decided to send her in the new year to an agricultural college for girls in Brittany. Meanwhile, after doing the morning chores in house and orchard, then feeding the rabbits and a goat, Agnès was free to go hiking or cycling with me.

I had invested in a bicycle so as to go flying down the hills to the town of Aix, where I was attending lectures in French language and literature. What a golden autumn ride it was, past rows of lombardy poplars lighting the green fields with yellow. Especially I loved the pink stucco walls of farmhouses with their red-tiled roofs and guardian cypresses. A season for adjectives! Thus gradually but deeply I fell in love with a Provence seen through double vision: my eyes and those of Agnès. Absorbed in the French way of life, fascinated by the characters I met *en pension*, I felt the leash that attached me to my Canadian family grow looser and looser. Yet I had no inkling of when or how it would break.

During that December and January period my sister, Sophie, was my confidante. Here is a passage from a letter:

January 25, 1930

I was eating my last Canadian apple when your letter arrived. Glad you are enjoying your course at last [at art school in Toronto]. Funny that you are so interested in Agnès, for she is very interested in you. Day before yesterday Madame S. [an American friend] and I were invited to lunch at La Havane. The day was ravishing, with sun and wind, and it seemed that I had forgotten the perfect glory of the hills and the view from the terrace. Agnès and I went picking narcissi and pervanches (nice name for periwinkles) and she confided to me her desire (often hinted at before) to visit Canada. Nothing I could say about its differences could disillusion her—she already adores it. Forests and rivers, lakes, mountains and prairies are singing in her mind. However (this is the pity of it), she hopes to save enough in 2 or 3 years to get there — and her allowance is two dollars a month!

Inevitably, January came, as did the time for Agnès's imminent departure for her agricultural school. By now she had become very attached to me – as if I were an older sister. However, one night in her Spartan attic room lit by a single candle she told me the story of her expulsion from the convent where she had boarded during her early teen years.

"We had to wear long black dresses with long sleeves, black stockings; attend Mass every day, rarely got out walking even in fine spring weather. Our studies were domestic: housecleaning, cooking, embroidery. I felt imprisoned! And I fell in love with a girl who suffered in the same way. Secretly at night we slipped into bed together, exploring our bodies. It was beautiful ..."

"And then?"

"The nuns found out and told us we were sinners and must do penance. I was enraged. I threw scenes. They sent me home."

As she revealed this suffering, whispering in the near dark, I felt compassion, but with warning signals of panic. She longed to caress me, but I had to tell her it was unwise, that I did not desire it. For that decision, Madame, her mother, would, I knew, approve of me. Yet how could she know that my "wisdom" was due to fear of the unexplored? The "free" Canadian girl was a novice, a late developer in physical sexual experience. My role as older sister, wise counsellor, continued to be played out with Agnès. My letter to Sophie elaborates:

February 18, 1930

I woke up rather late this morning, because it was dark; jumped up to throw open the shutters – and found it was snowing! That was enough to hurl my mind Clarkson-wards. Madame's children were very excited and ran up and down the hall shrieking the news to one another. But now, at noon, it has all disappeared, save for little white tufts on the tiled roofs.

Agnès left a week later than she expected because of repairs at her school. We talked a great deal, went for walks, had tea in my room up at La Terrace. But now I am condemned not to write to her, because of the very unfortunate result of all this intimacy. She is very passionate, you know, but innocent with it all. I was obliged to tell her a few things, and to attempt to banish her crush by making her ashamed of it. But time is the only remedy. It's a long story, but the same thing happened to her before, with another girl at school. The nuns separated them, forbade correspondence, etc. Ever since (until I came!) Agnès had been eating her heart out (exactly like a man) for fear the other girl should forget her. And she thought this intense, almost morbid preoccupation, was friendship. Sad, I've been through a siege. But I have made her think, and laid the seed of continency and reasonableness, I hope. But I don't know what she will do if she falls in love with a man. She will be so enflammée that he will shun her. I cannot give her wisdom – only experience will do that! I can only tell her she is too old now to get mixed up with a woman. It's funny, you know, but the poor child seems to possess all the passion her brothers I think lack. They are "war children"; without any "go" or ambition. They are of course not to be romantic as she; but she gets furious when Xavier tells her perfectly coolly that he intends to marry for money solely, like all his contemporaries. She remembers that her father and mother married for love, against the wishes of the grandmother de Lombardon, who from the day of the marriage (25 years ago) has refused to have anything to do with her son, his wife or their children.

Well; poor Agnès, treated at home like an overgrown baby, schooled in a convent, self-nourished on romantic novels – what will become of her? She has not the respect she should have for the noble business of marriage as practised in France. I told her she shouldn't fret, because she would be no more content with the American system where a girl floats from one lover's arms to another. It's true, she would be revolted, so I told her to stop reading novels and concentrate on the profession of horticulture she has chosen.

During the midwinter and spring months of 1930, I had moved to board at La Havane with Madame and her occasional pensioners. I was studying and beginning to write stories and the novella *Pavane*. As well, I attended French and Italian classes at the university, where I enjoyed friendships with English and European students. Always there was a letter from Agnès, a confessional love letter in which she began to *tutoi* me, a signal of deep intimacy. But as I remember I kept up the older sister role. And when we met once more, briefly, at Easter, she was more calm, more full of her activities out of doors, studying animal husbandry. I wondered, though, how she could make use of this knowledge when it came time to return to the small orchard acreage in Provence where young ladies were not supposed to be farmers. That closed circle of gentility and snobbery! That spinster aunt who painted her heart out in an attic studio – in between supervising her mother's household. "When young," I said, "she should have gone to Paris." Agnès knew it. Indeed, we both found some solace in sympathizing with the spinster aunt as representing the fate of creative women. But perhaps by some miracle of faith Agnès's own release came a few years before the war, when she met a young man who was a rebel from his own middle-class family. He was planning to enter the priesthood, but, like Agnès, fell madly in love.

For the rest of our lives – their lives and mine – we corresponded between the years and I visited them whenever I was abroad.

At the time of our first parting, however, I was gearing myself up to face the Imperial Press Conference in London that I would be attending with my father. I was very nervous and anxious for my future.

Two: London

I was terrified of what was to come, but I had definitely decided to leave Aix-en-Provence May 24, see Agnès the 25th, Paris the 26th and sail for England the 27th.

I still had to write the Alliance française examination to prove that I'd actually learned something. As I wrote to my father, I knew the profs at home wouldn't believe me if they made me speak. Quite hopeless. I hadn't received a compliment, and the French were (supposedly) polite.

It seemed there was no shaking my father from the fond illusion that I was a first-class student and should pursue postgraduate work. At Glen Mawr I had always stood first in my class, but only because my class was so small. For serious students, a memory for facts is indispensable, and I didn't think I had it. I suppose I had studied the French Revolution three or four different times. All I knew about it was that something had happened in 1789. A general idea of theories, yes, but nothing I could stick on an exam paper. Trying for a scholarship and then living on it afterwards would kill me, I thought. I would have no time to think or observe. I hoped that the following summer I could earn enough so as to take an M.A. at McGill. After that, I would teach in the west.

What would happen in London? I had been so bothered, ever since Christmas, about my ability to cope with life in England with JFB as guide at the Imperial Press Conference. Mother did not want to be one of the wives (or Father didn't want her to be!). It was apparently acceptable that a daughter take a wife's place – and indeed there was one other newspaperman from the west whose daughter would be in the Canadian delegation. Yet all those letters to and from Aix must have revealed my apprehension. The project was dizzying for me to contemplate, inexperienced as I was in meeting "society," and scornful of the rigid proprieties I would have to adhere to. So my first reaction was panic. Father's telegram read: "You are to go to Paris, take the train and ferry to Southampton where Aunt Dorrie will be there to meet you." Not only would I have to face unknown relatives, our three English aunts, but in London I was to be plunged into a high-society whirl. I was even to be presented to their majesties King George and Queen Mary.

In the bonny month of May, I had to say a hasty good-bye to Madame de Lombardon and the lyrical life as *pensionnaire* at La Havane. That villa had become a loved home. Madame seemed as distressed as I was and, come the holidays, Agnès would leave her agricultural school in Brittany only to find me gone. But it had to be lived through. Hire a jitney to Aix, a bus to Marseille, a couchette to Paris. Cherbourg would come next, then I'd go by ship to Southampton. Aunt Dorrie! How would I recognize my godmother?

It was a sunny morning with fluffy clouds, sparkling blue waves and my first view of England. As the ship drew into the dock, I looked with apprehension at the small knots of people gathered around piles of luggage. Choosing an empty spot by the ship's rail, I was conscious that I looked young and noticeable in my navy blue cape-style coat and my droopy felt hat. Near the gangway I saw a tall, fair, military-looking woman waving her hand tentatively. That must be Aunt Dorrie, I thought. It was. As I stepped ashore, we smiled and hugged. "I knew it was you, so French-looking in that hat and cape!" she said, taking my arm briskly as we walked towards the baggage depot. "Now we shall have lunch and then catch the ferry to Ryde." Ryde! My father had gone to public school in Ryde. Wasn't that near where Tennyson was buried? Or was it Swinburne? I began to quiver with excitement.

It only took a few hours for me to feel relaxed with Dorrie. She was remarkably attractive. Her haircut was Joan of Arc style, but permed; not waved or curled, but crinkly, light brown in colour. And she had those ruddy English cheeks, wide blue eyes. Her strong classical features filled me with admiration – even, perhaps, envy? I was able to talk to her frankly, but not too intimately, surprised at one point when she asked if I had ever been kissed. "Oh yes," I replied hesitantly, remembering a moonlit night in a canoe, a rubbery mouth pressing against mine. I had found the experience of petting most uncomfortable. "Oh, I do hope you were in love when you kissed." When I shook my head, she looked sorry. "Poor lamb." I remembered that her fiancé had been killed overseas. Like so many young women during the war, she went into war work and the women's army. There she met another lonely pal. They had lived together ever since. The same situation had caught our Aunt Ina, the artist, and Aunt Grace, the ex-governess who had taught English in Russia.

Dorrie, with her friend, ran a small nursing home near the sea on the Isle of Wight in the town of Shanklin. I cannot recall meeting any patients there, but the young doctor called round to see what could be done about my health. I had lost weight, had a fearful cold and was anaemic. So he prescribed iron injections and Dorrie made me sniff hot salt water up my nostrils and gargle. The sea air was invigorating, the food was wholesome, the sun shone every day as I walked about the neat, clean seaside town. I must have recovered fast, ready for the arrival of Father. We were to meet him in London just before the conference opened. He had seen to it that Dorrie would take me shopping for two days to outfit the poor little Canadian for the social life of London.

"Such a program!" she exclaimed, listing the conference events that the ladies would be expected to attend. These included the Lord Mayor's luncheon, dinner parties, the theatre, horse racing and a weekend in the country at one of England's great houses. In Kensington I was introduced to Swan and Edgar's and Harrod's, and fitted out with a tailored tweed suit; a three-quarter-length coat with hat to match (for Epsom); a black silk polka-dot suit, black felt cloche hat (for the Derby); a full-length flowered gauze dress and cape, with wide-brimmed black straw hat (for Ascot). There was also a pink tulle evening gown and another of white satin with a leaf-green silk shoulder bow. It was to be accompanied by a white ostrich fan (for dinner parties). Aunt Dorrie also supervised the accessories and the shoes, invariably too tight. "My," she said, "your father will be charmed with his lovely daughter." I began to take heart.

We were booked to stay at the Grosvenor, where JFB joined us. "Freddie!" cried Dorrie. He beamed and gave us each a hug. Dorrie was the youngest of his five sisters, the one who was a child when he had left the Isle of Wight for Canada. I was hoping she could stay longer, but she had her nursing home to attend to. I was left alone, very dependent on Dad's decisions.

The Imperial Conference opened on June 1, 1930, and I was soon caught up in a wave of appointments, with never a moment to myself. It began with breakfast in the hotel at eight, morning drives in a cab to leave calling cards, elaborate luncheons (gold plate at the Lord Mayor's Hall) with glasses of wines, in several sizes, that I barely sipped; conversation with the gentleman on the right, conversation with the gentleman on the left; afternoon sightseeing for the ladies, where Miss Corrigan, the girl from western Canada, and I were the only non-wives; then more receptions, followed by a lull for private dinner parties. I most enjoyed those where I could wear either the pink tulle or the white satin, waving my feather fan when the ladies rose from the table so as to leave the men with their port. With all this drinking, I just hoped JFB would be able to stay on the water wagon.

The most interesting of the dinner parties was at the home of Lady Jones, the novelist Enid Bagnold. How beautiful, how vivacious she was! And, strangely, she approved of Father and his shy Canadian daughter. While he and Sir John Roderick Jones talked shop, Enid Bagnold discussed books and plays. Plays? Of course I was taken to those, but later I could only remember *Bitter Sweet*, Noël Coward's musical with the song, "I'll See You Again."

During one formal dinner party at the horticultural gardens, I was seated between Margot Asquith and a younger member of the Churchill family. His first cousin was Randolph Churchill, the son of Winston. And because as a cub reporter I had interviewed the said Randolph for the *Toronto Star*, his name became a toothsome morsel for dinner conversation. I was doing all right!

What I hadn't known was that there was an orchestra set up in the zoo for dancing. All the young couples would spend the evening doing the fox-trot and tango, music that I loved but could not dance to. Inevitably my young dinner partner asked me for the first dance. I stood up awkwardly, moved out of time, then froze like a stiff hollyhock when the first frost hits. "Sorry," I murmured as he led me to a bench behind some tall ferns. He did not trouble to introduce me to any other young people in his coterie, but left me stranded. Suffering from a mixture of shame and fury, I got up and began pacing through the corridors, looking at botanical specimens. No sign of Father. So endeth the lesson.

By the time the next social event came along, I was still full of resentment over the rudeness of the British upper class. On learning that we were to go to the Tate Gallery, *not* to look at paintings, but to line up in a long reception hall to await the arrival of the Prince of Wales, I thought it was a ridiculous exercise. I had seen the Canadian women delegates practising their curtsies and I decided to ignore that ritual. As we stood there in two long lines, Dad somewhere on my side, Prince Edward came through the doors at the far end, surrounded by his entourage. Slowly he walked along, nodding from side to side. To my amazement his face, so often seen as that of a young man in the Canadian Press releases, was heavily wrinkled. In his naval gold-braid uniform he looked like an elderly doll.

Opposite me, members of the Canadian contingent began bowing and curtsying, but when he actually reached the spot where I was standing, I did not curtsy. Instead I gave him a wink. If he took note of it I could not tell. Impassivity was protocol. But he had certainly seen me. I was the youngest woman there. The fact that male members of the Canadian delegation later teased me about the wink did not trouble me a whit. I was able to laugh along with them. That was my first victory.

Was JFB aware of my skittish behaviour? He did not speak of it. But after another week of these London engagements (which included

listening to a rousing, flamboyant speech by Lloyd George), Dad
decided we'd had enough. "We won't take the trip to the north. You
couldn't be interested in mining or steel mills now, could you? Much
better to go to Portsmouth and visit the aunts – and on to the Isle of
Wight."

Alas for those plans. For no sooner had he made all the arrangements
with his sister than he received a telephone call from longtime family
friend Ruth Cohen, who had been widowed but was now married into
a literary milieu in London. She invited us to an evening at her
apartment "so Dorothy may meet Mr. Shaw." George Bernard Shaw!
One of my most admired writers. The hero whose heroines were Saint
Joan, Eliza Doolittle and Major Barbara. For me especially, his importance lay in his championship of women in his essays, *The Intelligent
Woman's Guide to Socialism and Capitalism.* To be able to return home
to fellow students at the University of Toronto, having met and talked
with the great man, was a dream almost too good to be true. It was
indeed too good.

Father said, "No, it is far more important for you to meet our family
and the town where I grew up. Cultivate your own roots."

"But you wanted me to meet writers! It was swell to be invited to visit
Enid Bagnold. And you told her I was a poet. It was you who got *Green
Pitcher* published and you boasted about it. Everywhere in Canada.
Can't you see how wonderful it would be for me to meet GBS?"

No, he couldn't see. On the trip to Portsmouth anger boiled within
me. The sailors' hotel looking out to sea held no charm for me now.
I went to my room early and tossed about all night. Father rapped on
the door to wake me up for early breakfast. Downstairs I was still sullen,
though I ate bacon, sausage, eggs and toast with undiminished appetite.
My father was occupied reading the morning paper, but finally he
peered over it to say, "Now I'll give you an hour or so till lunch before
we visit Ina."

"But what about the tour of Portsmouth? Do I have to go with you
today?"

"Such insolence. You are my daughter and you will behave as I see fit!"

Tears stung my eyes as I went upstairs to close my valise and put on my suit and hat. There would be time still to explore the waterfront. It wouldn't hurt Father if he had to wait a little.

I wonder, though, what possessed me? I made my way to the boardwalk and became fascinated observing the holiday crowd, listening to the different accents the British seemed to have, watching the sailboats tossing on a flashing blue sea, the sea gulls wheeling and crying. Every so often there would be a handy cove to poke about in, or, on the boardwalk itself, secluded alcoves where one could sit and have an orange drink with fish and chips.

I was wearing my wristwatch, but before I realized it the morning had gone by. It was noon. Now I decided it would take too long to walk back to the hotel in time for lunch. Why not pay a visit, as I had wanted to, all along, to Nelson's ship, *The Victory*?

I worked my way back through sightseers, found the entrance to the wharf, paid my shilling and did the tour of the ship. However, just as I was leaving for the street I felt a firm touch on my arm. Startled, I turned around. "I say, miss. Aren't you from Canada?" It was a bobby. Embarrassed, I was obliged to give my name and destination. "Come along with me then. Your father is that worried. We couldn't find you." I couldn't help smiling. But I began to feel more serious, guilty even, as we walked towards the hotel. There, hatless: a small, worried man. Shock set in when he hugged me, fiercely.

"Why? Oh, why?"

There was nothing to say. After, we both knew why. I had taken my first steps towards independence. There would be more to come. Perhaps none so painful.

In the meantime JFB had had to cancel the visit with his favourite sister, Ina, in Portsmouth. Instead, we would take the boat across to Ryde that very evening.

On Being in Love

It would seem that there are two kinds of sexual love a woman experiences. One is physical, the electric shock of touch; the other is mental, "the idea of the person." When these two forces are joined, when a woman can respond to both, in one man, then the experience is one of great wonder. But so often the problem is: "Either this, or that." Or else, given that the woman marries a man who provides full completion, familiarity tends to breed contempt. The "idea of the person" becomes somewhat worn out, threadbare: in daily living a new "person" emerges and what was simply the man's shadow takes on flesh, becomes his twin, his *doppelgänger*. This creature hangs around her neck! Perhaps therefore the happiest marriages may be those of the sailor or the fisherman, for absence revives the pristine image and when the man returns from his voyaging he is greeted as when he first came into her arms.

In my own experience of love this problem has been paramount. Too often I have been forced to choose between "either-or"; too often I have yearned for wholeness. Physical satisfaction without real love is the least to be desired. Invariably if a situation has started with the physical I begin to "fall in love," to seek the other as a person. And so, though there was a time when free love was much in fashion and marriage was too expensive, I have since found it wiser to forego having a relationship merely for the sake of sexual pleasure. When circumstances force a woman to live alone, the "ideal" love is the better. For

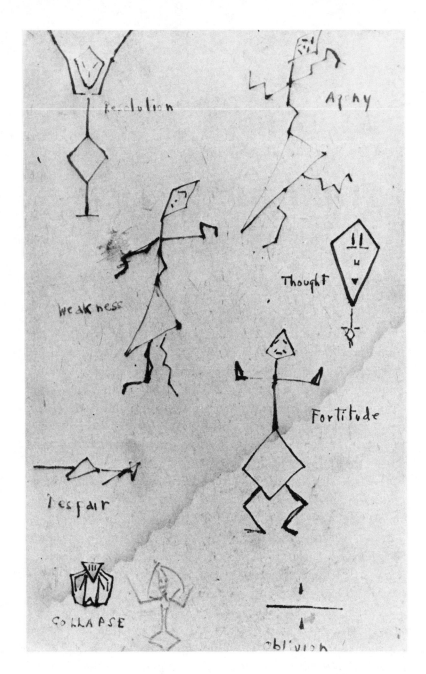

"DKL in love," a drawing done by the author ca. 1930

absence and abstinence, as Emily Dickinson and Charlotte Brontë could verify, are stimulants to passion. A woman *feels* beloved. Although she may be frustrated physically, she moves in happiness. Under such circumstances I believe she can be truly creative as an artist.

When I was a child myself, in those years between nine and twelve, I experienced the "ideal" love, but always for a boy older than myself. It was a kind of obsession. Any day that passed without my seeing him was a day weighed down. My fantasies about him were intense. Yet if he had come near, or spoken, or touched my arm, I would have been speechless with embarrassment.

The mental experience of love therefore came first, in my case, as is probably the situation with most human beings. But when I was thirteen or fourteen and again when I was nineteen, I had a fleeting experience with "touch." The first one was not with a boy my own age, but with a small child. There was a family of cousins with young children whom I used to look after sometimes. I remember that young Bobbie, about five years old, had elected to take me on a walk back of a farm in that farming country I loved, around Cooksville. I don't know why we two were the only ones going for a walk, but it must have been a fine spring day because I remember the dazzling new green leaves on the poplars, and the wind shaking them, and clouds running races up the sky. We ran too, Bobbie and I; and when I had stopped chasing him, he came to walk beside me and put his hand into mine. It was then that the shock came. An electric current, it seemed, passed from the pressure of his fingers against my palm, up through my arm, shaking my whole being. That sense of communication with another gave me a glimpse of what might come, sometime. I did not know how.

The next experience was equally unexpected, and more strange. I had come from France, in the spring of 1930, to visit my father's boyhood home on the Isle of Wight. We visited not only Ventnor, where his father, an architect, had designed some frightful Victorian gothic buildings, but also the environs, hiking all day long across the Downs, or along the cliffs to Shanklin via Sandrock Spring, where his aunt, the painter, had lived. And on most of these walks a relative, Pam, a year younger than I, came along with us. She was outdoorish, lean and sturdily built, dark-eyed and vivacious with that wonderful rose complexion that English girls possess. We had never met before but she looked up to me with some admiration, I suspect, because I was a Canadian and because I had been away from home and to a French university. Her enthusiasm for the family history and her love of the sea and the cliffs were as intense as my father's. On one of our excursions we ended up at a comfortable old inn set on a lonely headland. We stayed there the night. My father had a room to himself whilst Pam and I shared an upper bedroom, looking out to sea. After a British "tea" we were tired from the long day's hike and crawled into the double bed early. But we were no sooner in bed than we grew awake, alert, laughing and chattering as girls do. When finally there was a lull, Pam said softly: "I'm so glad you came, Dee." And she laid her hand on my belly.

Tremors seized me. Then they seized her. And before I knew it I was also stroking and caressing her limbs, her breasts; kissing her and leaning to hold her close, body to body. For me it was an utterly new sensation. I cannot speak for her, and I rather suspect that since she had come from an English boarding school she already knew something of these pleasures. But for me, heaven opened. I became aware that my body had always longed for another's body; that it experienced completion when touching the other. That was all: just a most delicate touching, pressing, caressing. Then it was over; we must, finally, have slept. In the morning we made no reference to it.

In the days following I had to come to terms with this experience. True, I had had "crushes" on older girls and teachers, when at a girls' school. But I had never, then, heard of lesbianism and I had never had any crushes where physical contact had been involved. I found I was not drawn to Pam as a person to be in love with. She was simply my cousin and my friend. There was not a deeper relationship, at least on my part. Did this mean I was "callow"? Did this mean, on the other hand, that

I would never be attractive to men? In another year's time I was to find out.

As I reread these passages I ask: is that the whole truth? And I am bound to say, no! For I do remember a short conversation with Pam the next day, in which she expressed her devotion to me and in which I (feeling older and wiser) advised her that we should forget about the night we had spent together: it was not a good thing. In saying this, I hurt her; I felt myself to be cruel. Yet I believe I took this stand from lack of understanding, lack of knowledge. Love is wisdom; and I had not enough love in me, then, to be wise.

The truth: all the truth! "Tell all the Truth but tell it slant," said Emily Dickinson. My father was more uncompromising: "If you can't tell the truth, shut up." It must be said, sadly, that the truth is cutting. It injures. All through my adolescence and my twenties I was more concerned with fighting sham, pretence, with "getting at the truth" about relationships with friends, teachers, parents, and with myself, so that I scorned the *bienséances*, the social niceties. I daresay I was a very objectionable young woman! Yet, because I was so hostile to the conformities of being well mannered I sought out similar souls. At school, Gina was one such, and during my second year at the University of Toronto, I met a student who seemed to me the first young man I had ever met who could talk freely and be utterly honest with me.

I shall call him Len. He was a second- or third-year student. He was probably repeating his year, so busy was he with extracurricular activities, especially journalism. The program and politics of the *Varsity*, the student newspaper, interested him intensely; and probably today he would be one of those in the forefront of student protest, a reporter-at-large, a radio haranguer. Even then he was as near "beatnik" as a man could be who came from a conservative, Anglican family. He acted on impulse, spoke out on impulse, scorned conformism and commercialism. As a result he was always broke, or borrowing, or in debt. Money meant nothing to him.

Therefore, just when I was at the stage of utter disgust with organized society, hating the university and longing for some contact with "reality" and for some person of the opposite sex who would not be conventional, who would not expect me to talk hockey, football or college gossip – just at that point, Len invited me to a formal dance at Trinity College. I had admired him from afar, at meetings of the *Varsity*. I liked his rough unslicked hair, his ruddy, clownish, humorous face, wide, loose mouth – all these aspects delighted me because they were not the conventional image of the student-about-campus. And although I had given up going to any student dances or social affairs because I was hopeless at dancing and even more hopeless at making conversation, nonetheless for some reason I was not apprehensive about going with Len. His grin was so disarming! And as it turned out, he was easy to dance with. He didn't seem to mind my bumbling feet, and he didn't have my program all booked up with strangers who would stiffen me. I think we spent most of our time standing about, talking, running hand in hand down corridors, climbing to the roof and looking over the city. It was to me an evening glorious and timeless as a dream because Len was not merely interested in all my views on society, on sex; he was "concerned" for me as a person. When I told him I hated university and wished I could see "the other side" of the city, get a job in a dress factory down in the Jewish quarter, he didn't look horrified, but replied simply: "Well, why don't you?"

And then, though the party was over, the dancers gone off in their cars, Len decided we could not go home yet: would I come downtown to Child's, the cafeteria restaurant, for some supper? This was "the thing" to do and I never dreamed I would be so invited. I was charmed. (It was only afterwards that I realized Len had no money for this event, and that he had left me alone for nearly half an hour while he went off rummaging for "a touch," I suppose.) I was still so far from being unconventional myself that I never thought of lending him the money. Indeed, he would not have taken it, not at that point in our relationship.

By the time we sat opposite each other in Child's (eating, I imagine, a huge ice-cream sundae), I was in such a daze of delight I knew that was it: I was in love! When Len drove me home my head leaned towards his shoulder; and when he stopped the car at the door he turned and very gently, softly, kissed me. In a dream I walked with him up the steps and said goodnight, formally. And he had gone.

It would have been good if that relationship, so happily begun, had developed. But for some strange reason I could not understand (though it gnawed at me all year) Len only invited me out one more time, to see a play at Hart House. My distress was great when my mother said I would not be able to go to the theatre, because she had arranged for me to go to a literary meeting with some friends of hers who wanted to meet "the young poet." I did not openly rebel, but I had to tell Len this. He got me two tickets for the play, for Saturday night, but he regretted he could not go with me, as he would be out of town that weekend.

Any girl among my friends and acquaintances who was not asked out again by a young man would have given up, decided that the shadow was already "booked" or that he was not really attracted. I couldn't believe any of those possibilities! I was sure we were kindred souls; I was sure he had felt as happy as I did. And so, for an entire year, I spent my days looking for Len, trying to catch sight of him in the distance, hoping to speak to him, yet not knowing what to say when he did stop for a conversation. He seemed just as sympathetic as ever, just as genuinely interested, not in the least constrained as a young man would be who did not want the attentions of a woman poet. Yet he never spoke of our relationship! Out of those silences I wrote the poems in *Signpost*. They were not published until a year after I graduated and by that time Len was married, with a baby. He had been engaged to a farmer's daughter all along. But even my closest friend in that university circle, who knew it, had not told me. Why aren't women loyal to their friends?

Still another "ideal" relationship of those years was my friendship with Raymond Knister, the Ontario imagist poet. Curiously enough, the very first time I had a conversation with him about poetry, sitting in front of the fire at 132 Walmer Road in Toronto, was the day when

I was preparing to go out to that dance with Len. So my mind was distracted. Knister told me years later that on that day he had wanted to follow on and make me his lover, but he felt that could be taking advantage of my youth. He wanted a wife and a home, but I was not yet fledged! He was right in a way. But it is certain I would have grown up much faster and perhaps have been more wholly devoted to one man, had he been bolder. Like my father, he was quite shy; like my father, he stuttered abominably.

It is certain that I was drawn to Raymond. I can remember feeling a very strong sensation of empathy in thinking about him, what I called "electricity." It was as if I could hear his voice saying my name. And I replied with "Raymond! Raymond!" But by the time I met him again he was married with a daughter, Imogen; and I was still passionately loyal to the man I had been living with in Paris, Tony.

But to go back a year in time, to the end of my fourth year at U of T. The end of my fourth year was traumatic, in a sense. I had had a glorious time, my only year of real fun and laughter. But I had failed to do brilliantly in my honours course (French and Italian), achieving only a second-class; and I had failed to relate to the opposite sex. It seemed as if every man who liked me met Gina and was drawn to Gina more! Although she was undoubtedly as egotistical and therefore as unable to reach towards a young man as I was – to understand him, that is, and be some support to him – nonetheless she was an exotic creature, a "femme fatale" as we liked to put it, à la Michael Arlen's novel *The Green Hat*. Men could not keep away from her. By contrast I was dreamy and remote. Then Gina went off to Europe with Professor Otto van der Sprenkel, insisting that I plan to come to Europe too. My idea was to go to the Sorbonne and continue my studies in comparative literature – French and English contemporary poetry – but at first my father would not hear of it. He felt that I should have won a scholarship to go, and that I should get a job. However, by that year, 1931, a situation looked hopeless for a graduate in arts. With an M.A. behind me, I argued, I might have a better chance getting into a university as a lecturer. I decided to await developments and earn some money for my passage by running a coffee shop during summer school (I have published a description of Charlotte's in my book *Right Hand Left Hand*).

Throughout my last year I had been meeting some of the young men who had graduated from the *Varsity* staff and had gone into newspaper work, some with Canadian Press, others on local newspapers. Such were Nathaniel Benson, Paddy Ryan and others. This was a much "tougher" crowd than the university people I had known. Their main interest, weekends, was drinking and having parties. They each had a girl, more or less permanent, and I drifted somehow into being the girl who went with one I shall call Hugh. He was a very different sort from the students I had known: older, from the prairies, he had known the rough-and-tumble of making his own way. Yet he was very interested in politics, as I was beginning to be, and had studied some of the theories of the United Farmers, the OBU (One Big Union) and finally of the CCF. Hugh's problem was that he was inarticulate; rather clumsy, ungainly, he was often tongue-tied. He was twenty-eight or twenty-nine when I knew him, just a reporter on a country-town paper who had drifted aimlessly, wanted to settle down with a girl perhaps, but had no "dash." Rather, his virtues were the hidden ones of solidarity and loyalty. He was a man of silences, yet there was poetry in those silences. I sensed something of this, but though I liked Hugh very much as a friend, I felt no infatuation, no physical pull towards him. It was therefore a surprise to me (as well, I think, to him) that we began to spend those early summer weekends together; he took me to supper dances and canoeing on the Humber River. He was deferential to anything I took it into my head to do. And so eventually, one night in our empty Toronto house, I took it into my head that I wanted to explore sex, deeply, and for the first time, and he was the one who could best guide me. He was surprised, taken aback, and I was completely unaware that a deflowering presented dangers to the male.

Strangely, it was a kind of pre-wedding night. "May I come up?" he asked. As in the initiations where the shaman is assigned to deflower the virgin, I went upstairs and undressed, lay on the only available double bed and covered myself with a sheet. Then he followed and slipped in beside me. I was trembling, but he soon quieted that. Then he pressed into me. After that we hardly slept at all. It was the opening for me of a whole new world of sensation and wonder, which I recorded much later in the poem "Comrade." At one point, I remember he was hungry. We ran downstairs naked, only to find oranges in the icebox but nothing else. No steaks! However, he contented himself with the oranges. Then, as we looked outside at the soft grey dawn coming, we saw that it was beginning to rain. "Let's go out in the rain!" I don't know who said it; it could have been either one of us; we were moving so harmoniously together that whatever happened it was one rhythmic movement. So we ran out naked into the arms of the sleeping city, into the back garden under the elm trees and stood there laughing, letting a mist of rain fall on us. Then he laid his hand on my flank, and we turned as one person and ran up to bed again.

That was how I "lost my virginity." I was twenty.

I didn't see Hugh after that, until he came with the Charlotte's crowd to the train station to see me off to Paris. He had wanted me to stay on in Canada, and I might have done so, had he been an aggressive type of man, pursuing me relentlessly. But I would have resented that. I would have longed for the freedom to be on my own, away from home. He must have guessed that I was not in love with him. What he did not know was the debt I owed him, for I never lost the knowledge that ecstasy was possible in the communion created by the union of two bodies. I came to realize that for some human beings these bodies could be of the same sex: but for me at that time they had to be male and female, each one taking turns at domination and passivity, each one searching how to become human.

Strange Encounter: Raymond Knister

My memoir about Raymond Knister – his life, his work, his death by drowning – was published in 1949 by the Ryerson Press as an introduction to his collected poems, which I edited. That volume is hard to come by now. Even when it was printed, so long after that day on Lake St. Clair when the swimmer disappeared, even then no one knew for sure whether it was an accidental or a planned drowning. This dilemma led my editor, Lorne Pierce, to ask me for an account of Raymond's state of mind when I had last talked to him in early August of 1932. "I wish I knew why he died," wrote Pierce. He then told me that he had offered Knister hope of an editorial position with the Ryerson Press. Later, while at his summer home, Dr. Pierce received an urgent letter of which he wrote:

His latest letter sounded so desperate that, when it was forwarded to me at camp, I took the next train to Toronto, feeling that no man should suffer like that without all the help I could give him. I arrived only to learn that he had been drowned.

Apparently in early August Knister had come to Toronto alone in order to search for a publishing job that would support his family but leave him time enough for writing a third novel. He must have called on Frederick Philip Grove, Bertram Brooker, Mazo de la Roche and my mother, among others. That was how I came to meet him again, after many years, at Woodlot. I was holidaying there since my return from Paris. I had first known him in my teens when he came to our house to discuss his poetry. Now he wanted to discuss mine. We all had tea together in the garden at Woodlot, during which Raymond explained that he was on his way to Toronto. I clapped my hands. "Just where I want to go," I told him. So we set off, in his old bus, along the lakeshore road. His stammering seemed to have improved and he began plying me with questions as to my views on poetry and the writing game.

What I had to tell him was that I had undergone a new direction in my thinking, and was solely interested in writing that possessed social or revolutionary significance. Raymond expressed himself as astonished, though not shocked, and proceeded, hammer and tongs, to find out why I believed poetry should deal with movements and messages, when all these things were transitory. Seeing I was adamant, he changed his tack and related that while living in Detroit he had become interested in the working-class movement and in factory life. He had even written a novel about it, he said. Often he had talked with Leo Kennedy and his socialist crowd in Montreal and had some sympathy with their views, politically. But what had any of this to do with poetry, he demanded? Poetry must concern itself with an individual response to the beauty and sorrow of the world.

I disagreed; was scornful of him as a bourgeois; I felt that it was too bad Raymond was so far behind the times. When he told me what he was trying to write – Henry Jamesian short stories – I was even more cool.

He persisted, however, with the idea that he wanted me to see them and criticize them. He suggested we stop at Sunnyside and enjoy watching the beach and the bathers. But I was heading for a dinner engagement and not to be deterred. Raymond insisted on driving me home. He would bring over his stories the following day. I agreed, suggesting that if I was not home he could leave them in the letter box.

I went out for the evening, into the university area, for supper and to a meeting on Marxist literature. Afterwards, I came home alone by streetcar. No sooner was I in the house and upstairs taking off my sweater and skirt when the doorbell rang. Surprised, I hastily pulled them on again and went to open the door. There stood Raymond.

"I – I – thought I would bring you this manuscript tonight," he stuttered.

"Thank you very much." And before I could say anything further he had invited himself into the hall, closing the door.

He passed a few remarks of no significance, still standing in the hall, and then I asked how he knew I was home. "I just got in," I said.

"I know," he said. "I followed you."

"What?" I responded.

He confessed he had watched me depart from the house and had later waited at the streetcar stop until I returned. He then came along to the house after me.

I was nonplussed. But even more so when he said: "It's because I know now you are the only woman. I love you."

Well, I challenged that. Pointed out that he scarcely knew me, had met me under half a dozen times and had altogether different views from mine.

"I have always known you," he said. "Always loved you. Ever since you were a young girl."

"Then why didn't you say so? And why did you marry?"

"Because you were too young. I could not dare interfere with your life at that point. Fifteen, weren't you?"

This weakened me considerably. He must have sensed this, because he followed it up with the question: "Did I mean anything to you – ever?" I admitted (foolishly) that when I was sixteen or seventeen I was in love with him, with that remote love a girl has for a remote ideal. Had he seen more of me at that time I might have become deeply involved. Instead, he passed out of my ken and I fell in love with Len who, if no more receptive than Knister at the time, fully occupied my emotional life.

But once I had admitted to an interest in him there was no holding Raymond back. (That stubbornness has been noted by others who knew him intimately.) He insisted I was the ideal woman whom he had always loved and that the time had now come for us to meet and become one. It developed that what he meant by this was not any gradual friendship or courtship, but an immediate going to bed together. In order to divert him from this idea which did not appear attractive to me, I plunged into the subject of his marriage and of sex in general. Particularly D. H. Lawrence's views of it. Raymond had read *Sons and Lovers,* but not *Lady Chatterley's Lover.* This I promised to lend him.

In the course of this discussion – still in the hall, as I had found that one movement towards sitting down in the drawing room with him was too dangerous; he was literally gasping to get me down beside him – he told me that he had made the great mistake of remaining a virgin until his marriage at twenty-eight. He had had no idea what sex would mean to him and he had been almost overwhelmed by it. On the other hand his wife had no similar response. She remained frigid and quite unable to feel the sensations he felt, or to participate actively with him.

"Well?" I said, sharply. "If your wife is frigid it is no one's fault but your own. Any psychologist would tell you that."

He refused to accept the idea. No! When first married, though she would not discuss the sexual act or any sensation she might have, his wife did say that it was like a kiss. He apparently longed to have her declare an excitement and surge of activity similar to that he felt, but she never seemed to respond. How could the sexes ever be equal, he demanded, if women were not as active as men? If participation was not mutual? He felt that there must be a woman who was capable of participation.

I suggested *Lady Chatterley's Lover* again. I went to fetch it for him, gave him the book, edging him towards the door.

"Look here," he said. "You must understand. I must be with you. Can't you see it isn't just the body I am asking for? I could go downtown in my car and pick up a woman anytime. It's not that. It's you!"

Since he would not accept the fact that I had no desire for him, I then found that the only reason for refusal I could give was to tell him I loved someone else. This was true, though I was not engaged or bound to the other person. Even that did not deter him. "You're just being coy," he said, and tried to pull me towards him, and into the drawing room. This made me furious as well as making him appear ridiculous. In order to stay on talking, he plunged into other matters – his agonies of mind and indecisions about the nature of the world and the nature of the creative writer. He felt he wanted to save me from my errors in choosing the materialistic philosophy of revolution. I was a person who must remove myself from the world and just create.

"I know of a place, a cabin, up in northern Ontario. That's where we could go together, and grow away from the world and into the nature of things. We could really write."

"What would we live on?" I asked him. "And what about your wife and child? Surely you have assumed responsibility towards them? Surely you cannot evade it?"

He brushed this aside. His wife was no longer a real wife to him, she did not participate in union with him. He was sure he could prove to me that ours would be a perfect relationship.

After about two hours of this tense, excited talk, backed by his fanatical determination that I was merely holding out on him, I finally opened the door and insisted that he go. We had a brief tussle on the verandah, during which I dropped the key on the steps.

"Oh, hell," I said, dashing to retrieve it.

"Oh, hell," he repeated emphatically, trying to catch and embrace me. I shook him off, went in and closed and locked the door. Then I went to bed. I felt too shaken to sleep for hours. And so by morning I was in a dead slumber.

Somehow, the doorbell awakened me. I stumbled up, sleepily putting on my dressing gown and looking at the clock. It was 8:00 A.M. I went downstairs, opened the front door, and there he stood.

This time I felt really angry, but he did not appear to be aware of it. He had stayed up all night, he said, pacing his room and reading *Lady Chatterley's Lover*. There was nothing in it of what he was seeking. D. H. Lawrence's women were only a little more alive; they nevertheless remained passive, never really experiencing what it was possible for a woman to experience.

I disagreed with him, to no avail. He wanted to experiment with me, then and there. He had gone to the drugstore and bought the necessities.

His actions seemed so fantastic, so removed from reality that I began to pity him, to wish I could be of any help. But there seemed to be no way. He would accept no compromise. So I had to tell him that I was going to dress and go out to a café for breakfast and then go to a friend's place. I phoned my mother in Clarkson to reassure myself and repeated with marked emphasis the fact that she was coming into town that morning. Raymond listened, resignedly. He stayed quietly downstairs while I dressed. Then we went out of the house silently and he drove me to a St. Clair Avenue café. I did not even ask him to breakfast, too afraid that he would interpret the move as a relenting gesture.

That was the last I saw of him. I read his stories dutifully, did not like them and said so in a letter sent to Port Dover. He replied a week later, in a perfectly calm way, urging me, at some length, to study Keats's philosophy and point of view on the poet. He closed by asking if I would visit them in the country, whenever I could manage it.

Two weeks after I had seen him, I was in Montreal visiting with Leon Edel and his mother. The telephone rang; it was Leo Kennedy. Leon broke off to turn and tell me, "Raymond Knister is dead – was drowned today."

I remember screaming out, "I killed him, I killed him." I believed
then his death was not an accident, and my first reaction was one of
guilt. Leon hastily finished his conversation with Kennedy and turned
to hear my story. He tried to put some sense into me and to assure me
that if it was suicide – for which there was no proof – the man himself,
wrought up and obsessed as he was, was responsible. I might have been
a small link in the chain that led to the finality.

The story of Raymond's death is as follows: He was on an
unplanned holiday at Lake St. Clair with his wife and small daughter.
One afternoon, he went to the shore for his usual swim. His wife was
too busy to accompany him, as had been customary. Raymond took
the rowboat out some distance from the shore. Before Myrtle and wee
Imogen, watching from their cottage, could believe it, he had disappeared, his body seemingly sucked down by an undertow. It took
three days of dragging to find him.

If he was obsessed, he was obsessed with the idea that he was a great
poet and that to join the immortals he must renounce all the ties of life
that bind and enslave the creative artist. His spirit could then be free
but it would be bound to earth through the intercession of those who
loved him. Such would be Rilke's interpretation.

Whether his spirit actually possessed me, or whether the violence of
his going made me feel burdened, I do not know. I do know that I was
freed from him only a year later when, returning from work in New
Jersey, I went to spend a week alone on an Ontario farm. I wrote the
poem "The Outrider" for Raymond, and dedicated it to him. Then, for
a time, I let him go. Or he let me go.

Fifty years have passed since my last encounter with Raymond Knister.
Since then much has been written about him – his life and his work –
and there remains conflicting evidence as to whether he was acciden-
tally drowned or whether the tensions of his life led him towards
suicide. In 1987 I published an article about Raymond in *Books in*

Canada. It created quite an uproar, and as a result I wrote to my long-time friend Leon Edel, both as a biographer and as someone who had known Raymond, asking for his opinion about the possibility that Knister's death was not an accident. He replied with the following appraisal:

I have read your memoir of Knister very closely and with a kind of double eye: first with memories of our old friendship, and second with the eye of a professional biographer. It is the latter who is speaking to you now. I think it is a beautiful memoir, very moving, deeply felt, and there are moments of tenderness and insight in your most characteristic vein. But the data is inconclusive. I do not see any marked depression. I see only the discouragements that all writers had in Canada at that time – it was a small country, it was a small reading public, it was very hard to find publishers, and I am sure that even today conditions are far from ideal. Indeed, in the United States, with all its wealth, writers have a very hard time. And their earnings in the present inflation are starvation earnings – except for the best sellers, and the pornographers. Knister's identifying himself with Keats and Shelley is psychologically interesting, but it is not at all clear that he identified himself with their early deaths except in that one bit of testimony from Myrtle. But it doesn't prove anything. So speaking in a hard objective way one might speculate that there may have been a death wish, Shelleyesque – death by drowning – but one would have to know how good a swimmer he was, and whether he didn't have a cramp, and whether as he swam his unconscious took over, so that he was not as alert as he should have been. If there was an undertow, that was not necessarily a rendezvous with death. It was probably an accident. So one would need more evidence – seen with all the possible alternatives, and seen in the light of someone who was striving to succeed but who had indeed the challenge of the Canadian situation of that time. And he had a lot of fight in him.

I accept these findings. Alongside, however, I must reassert the fact that in August 1932 Knister was without a house to live in and without an income. His letter to Lorne Pierce was "so desperate" that Pierce left his Muskoka cottage so as to reach Toronto and offer Knister an editorial job. Pierce accepted my view that it was lack of any financial security that had the young poet blocked. There were no Canada Council grants then, nor, it would appear, was Knister receiving any financial assistance from his family.

Raymond Knister was undeniably a victim of the thirties' Depression and, until it was too late, no one understood. Of all the legacies Raymond Knister has given Canada, the best is the least ambitious: the collection of his poems. If they have a purpose it can be expressed in this quotation from Rilke's *Die Aufzeichnungen des Malte Laurids Brigge,* his favourite:

Verses are not sensations, as people think — they are experiences. For the sake of a single verse one must see many towns, men and things, one must know the animals, one must feel how the birds fly, and in what way the little flowers open in the morning.

Consequences

In the Montreal of 1933–34 Maysie Roger and I were plunged into a world of stress and confusion. We were apprentices with a Protestant family agency that delivered welfare vouchers to unemployed families. Applicants would go to the front office for an initial interview. Then, if the need was felt to be legitimate, cases would be assigned to area workers. That meant a house visit, an interview with questionnaire in hand, an attempt to sympathize with the clients' problems, social and emotional as well as immediate and realistic: a week's supply of coal gone too soon, electricity cut off, rent overdue with threats of eviction, hungry children, no carfare. For Maysie and me, young WASPs, it was not only a physical shock to see poverty face to face, it was a psychic shock. This situation made me all the more committed to doing away with the capitalist system, whereas Maysie, coming from a sheltered Ottawa education, did not want to get involved with political protests, let alone action in the streets. The result, under-standably, was that between us there were frequent, sometimes impas-sioned arguments after we had climbed the stairs with our groceries to share the kitchen tasks. Maysie, I think, was afraid of the bursts of anger that she was likely to meet with from her frustrated clients. People ought to take things philosophically, reasonably, calmly – or so she had been taught.

To Maysie's credit, she was not judgmental in her relations with me; indeed she was generous, never objecting to me having political meetings in our small sitting room cum kitchenette, where I had a cot for sleeping. She seemed content to have the refuge of a bedroom-study where she could retreat. I am afraid, though, that my comrades from the communist underground never thought of lowering their voices. So Maysie joined a group of music lovers, recorder players, who met on the same nights as did my political unit.

Actually, my real interest was in the theatre. In Paris I had been fascinated by Brecht's influence on guerrilla theatre. With Tony I had marched to Père-Lachaise, the cemetery where the 1870 Communards were buried. Along that route had appeared *les blouses bleues* who with their chants cheered the marchers on. In Montreal that memory encouraged me to try writing "mass chants" and practising with group voices.

Although we did perform a few times at trade union meetings, I was still timid about participating in public places. I particularly remember getting up at 5:00 A.M. one wintry day so as to be part of a strikers' picket line beside a steel mill. Back and forth, back and forth we walked, brandishing slogans and talking *en français* with the workers. After doing my stint (quite nervously) I caught a bus back to the welfare office. Not arrested! Montreal, that winter, was seething with political upheavals, but the only section of the city that I knew was the Jewish and Protestant enclave between St-Denis and St-Laurent. The French-Canadian unemployed came under a different welfare administration. My impression was that they were under the aegis of the Catholic Church, and that they were politically naive and unorganized. I did visit one Huguenot family, a charming old couple sympathetic to the Soviet Union. They were disillusioned when I lent them my copy of *And Quiet Flows the Don* by Sholokhov.

My particular comrades were young men and women of European descent working in the needle trades. Their heroes would have been Sam Carr and Fred Rose, rather than Ontario's Leslie Morris and Tim Buck. I remember that in our unit, Joe, the son of a Jewish tailor, pleaded that he would have to drop out of the party because his wife was going to have a baby. She was becoming very nervous about his underground activities. I sympathized with him, but the other members, mostly solid married couples, were scornful. They put the party first. *They* had no babies.

No babies. That was the general rule we had to face up to. If we were to do useful political work – preparing and distributing pamphlets, picketing, organizing unions, rallying at meetings – we could not be tied down to nurturing children. Moreover, on the seven dollars a week that a party organizer earned, how could he or she afford to be a parent? The rest of us had precarious jobs.

While I had always thought of myself as a lover of children and a potential mother, that role would have to be reserved for the future. In the meantime: how to find a mate, yet prevent conception? In our student days Gina and I had learned a good deal about birth control from the lectures of Emma Goldman and the books of Marie Stopes. In Paris, with Tony, I had successfully used the chemical cone. But now, in Montreal, the French safe was the only easily available contraceptive method. We knew nothing of the rhythm method practised by some Catholics, nor of withdrawal, which I consider a cruel experience for women. Indeed, for me, so wonderful was the act of becoming as one, body to body, that I tended to ignore mechanical techniques. The year before I had been near despair at losing Tony. I was still empty, missing him. So when a young comrade in my unit, Don, began walking me home through the snowy streets of the inner city, I found it natural and inevitable to invite him to my warm flat for "a cup of tea and a bun." Maysie would be fast asleep in her room. We talked in whispers and were soon comforting each other, body to body, all sadness dissolved.

Don was Anglo-Saxon, the son of a mill worker. He had only a grade-school education. He found it difficult to write, or to speak up, but he was eager to learn. I noticed that he was very responsible in carrying out political tasks. I was not in love with him, but his gentleness and kindness made him a true friend. When the inevitable happened that spring, and I found myself pregnant, both of us were dumbfounded. "You mean I could be a daddy?" he queried. "You can't be," I said. "It can't happen. You have no job, or hope of jobs."

I set about finding a friend who could advise me what to do. This was none other than Louis Kon. That genial, teddy-bearish man was like an indulgent uncle to me. It was my first encounter with a member of the Russian 1905 intelligentsia, Gorki's generation. Louis and his Belgian wife immediately knew what doctor to send me to – a recently graduated MD who verified that I was pregnant. He tried the winding approach – tying me up inside – but it did not work. So, as I was finishing my apprenticeship in Montreal and was due to start at a real job that June in Toronto, he gave me the name of a Toronto doctor, a member of the party, who I was to see as soon as possible. At the same time he told me frankly that I was not sex crazy, but I needed marriage.

Back in Toronto, at my parents' house, 20 Rosemount, my worst anxiety was in not knowing how much an abortion would cost. I knew that my father had helped a young male cousin of ours to pay a heavy sum for his girl's abortion. Now, at a preliminary interview with Comrade Doctor, I asked him what the price would be. He was a spare, tight-lipped man, not given to explanations. "It's for the party," he said. "Forty dollars." At that I smiled weakly. He did inspire confidence – and was he not helping women at the risk of losing his profession? His life, even.

I guess it was a sign of mutual maturity in our relationship that I was able to tell JFB of my predicament and he was able to offer help: "But we won't tell your mother." That summer my parents were living at Woodlot. I told my father the date of my appointment. It was to be in the evening, a time when the small medical building would be closed. Of course the doctor had his keys. He would let me in, then drive me home to Rosemount Avenue.

I was alone; neither Gina nor Lon was allowed to come with me to the appointment. I had qualms, of course, and the surgeon's manner was not too reassuring. But, having got this far, I had to go through with it. After examining me he said, "This will hurt." He could not give me any anaesthetic or shots so it did hurt – to the point of my screams. I had never known such pain. He put a towel in my mouth, saying, "Nearly over now." Soon he was helping me get off the bench. I was trembling, fumbling with my clothes. He turned to the basin to wash his hands, his gloves, then took the crook of my arm and walked me down the office stairs. By then it was dark outside. His car was parked in a back lane. In silence he drove me home. "Wear a napkin," he instructed. "Stay in bed tomorrow."

Alone upstairs I panicked. I telephoned my father. "It's done," I said. "But I'm scared. Can you come?"

"Right away."

"Good. Tell Mother I have a fever." And so they came. In the morning Gina and Lon visited, closed my bedroom door and helped with the bedpans. They had to tell my mother that I was having a hemorrhage and should stay absolutely quiet. Inevitably, she insisted on calling our family physician. In those days people didn't rush to hospital, for which I was thankful, and I knew this doctor well enough from childhood to tell him the truth. Such a small, fussy man, I thought.

"Why didn't you come to me directly – weeks ago?"

"I didn't think you'd approve. I had to do this."

"I respect my patients' trust," he said, then added, cunningly, "Who is this abortionist fellow?" Of course I would not tell him. I would not give him a clue. "Well, it's all over for you now. Lie low. See me next week."

A month or so later the family allowed me to have a weekend party at Woodlot. The invited were all young communists – university students, artists, writers. We had a potluck supper, then sat on the floor in the many-windowed living room, a fire glowing in the large stone fireplace. Led by a comrade just returned from Russia, we sang Russian folk songs, with a few IWW – Industrial Workers of the World – rousers thrown in. In the morning my friends packed their sleeping bags and set off through the woods for the railway station. The tallest, best-looking, most sophisticated comrade stopped a moment to thank the Livesays for their hospitality. My father shook his hand, but as they disappeared down the path he asked me, sotto voce, "Was he the one?"

"No," I smiled sadly. "That one lives in Montreal."

Crossing the Border

Maybe it was a sort of game, my year in Montreal and the following one in Englewood, New Jersey. I was thrusting myself body and soul into politics, likely to assuage the pain of my lost love affair. Be that as it may, Montreal had been intriguing just to think about – to be able to speak French again, perhaps, and to study the whole social scene that was in upheaval against Quebec's repressive government.

I had more to learn, however, the next year, 1934-35, when I followed Gina and Lon – now legally married – to try out my fortune as a social worker in the United States. New York! What that metropolis meant to us, as undergraduates, was the opportunity to see European films like *Dr. Caligari, Sous les toits de Paris* and *Sang d'un poète.* A dozen of us would pile into a bus, riding all night just to spend two days filled with films, concerts and plays. I yearned for the excitement of the city. Stacked against me was the fact that I was a loyal member of the Communist Party and was not going to the U.S. to forget it. So how was I to get over the border?

I simply took a bus and was waved through, as a visitor. In the station I phoned the Lawsons for directions to their apartment in the village. Then I bought a paper. Whew! The first news that caught my eye was that the service staff of Macy's department store was on strike and would be demonstrating that afternoon. What a quandary. I should be on the picket line, but if I got picked up and put in the paddy wagon I could be sent straight back to Canada and, of course, to Father.

Well, there was a picket line and I marched, but on the far inner edge, near the department store windows. The police pulled up, seized a young woman to the left of me. I shrank back, window gazing, and the police, their van filled with salesgirls, moved on up the street.

My first attempt at a job in New York City was answering an ad from a fish cannery. On the telephone the man told me I'd have to get up at 5:00 A.M. and be on the other side of the city by 6:00. The wages were quite low and the hours long. The Lawsons certainly discouraged me from doing that sort of work. Next I applied to an agency that provided opportunities for social workers. One position was close to the city, the other was in a community centre across the Hudson River in Englewood, New Jersey. I decided to apply to the latter and was immediately granted an interview with Miss White, the director of Memorial House. Miss White turned out to be a New Englander quite interested in Canada; she was also concerned that I would be open-minded when working with a coloured community. (In those days, I used the term "Negro" but soon learned to say "coloured." No one used the present-day term "black.") I told the director that I'd worked in Montreal with various ethnic groups and that I would be keen to have similar experiences. She hired me on the spot.

As well as serving a coloured community, Memorial House had a caseworker who dealt with white families. Another social worker was Joan, who was responsible for athletics, sports and health care. In addition, there was Luella, a black caseworker responsible for services to her own part of town across the tracks. High on the hill lived the well-to-do whites.

How different was the American scene. In Canada, political tension was high and anyone with left-wing tendencies was suspect. One had to move as on a tightrope. The difference in the U.S. was the fact that Roosevelt was president and had established the National Reconstruction Administration. I was very impressed with what Roosevelt was doing about the unemployed. Instead of handing out welfare cheques or setting up food banks as we still do, he encouraged progressive programs – not only economic ones such as the great Boulder Dam experiment, but also projects that gave power to local communities to beautify the cities. Artists, sculptors, architects, even musicians and writers began to get jobs, as well as industrial workers. Consequently, in communities such as Englewood, the only people truly in need of help were middle-class families. Whether that was true all over the country I would not know, but certainly I did visit families who lived on the "white" side of the tracks and had never before been obliged to face poverty. I soon became aware, since I was working in the community as a caseworker, that there were specific social problems to be faced: housing, overcrowding, unemployment – all affecting the hundreds of black people who were moving or had moved from the south into small towns around New York.

I was not responsible for dealing with the black families, but I did have cases where I was concerned about a white girl involved with a black youth. I also saw the poverty the blacks had to endure when the schoolchildren in our neighbourhood came to Memorial House for a hot lunch of pork and beans. But my main knowledge of the situation came from talking with my fellow social workers. In particular, I enjoyed the company of Joan, who came from a well-established New England family. She worked alongside Luella. Also on the staff was a university-educated black man, Paul. From these three I got to know how stifled and impoverished was the black population.

Another person I got to know was an interesting, tough little fellow named Scotty. Broad Glasgow accent, bandy legs, sparse greying hair; he had a genuine gentleness about him, lit up by sparks of humour that delighted me. Scotty was an ardent nonpractising Jew whose best friend was a young rabbi with socialist inclinations. It was a pleasure for me to be able to talk politics with both of them. Sometimes we joined up with Joan and Paul when we were in the common room together after evening programs.

Further afield, we had one fascinating evening in Harlem, listening to jazz in a bar and watching the dancing. In Englewood of course we could never have done this; we could never be seen together in a car, three whites and two blacks. We began then to talk about racial prejudice, which I had found so noticeable. Luella and Scotty felt they didn't have any and I also claimed to be pure. But Paul was of a different belief. In a restaurant he let us talk away, arguing across the table. He leaned towards me, challenging me about being free of prejudice. "Why," he said, "you wouldn't marry me, now would you?" "Well yes, I would ... if I was in love with you." "If!" he repeated. He thought this was not a true answer at all. It was clear to me anyway that Paul and Joan were much attracted to each other; it was as if he were asking the question of Joan.

It was perhaps not that night, but some other talking time the following week, when Paul told me of his family background in the south. He had had an uncle who was hanged on a tree by the Ku Klux Klan. Small wonder the family moved north, enabling Paul to get some education at the high-school level. He had such good reports during his first college years that he determined to become a lawyer. He therefore applied to a university in the north where no blacks had ever been admitted. Because Paul had a surname the same as that of a prominent Englewood family, he sent his application without enclosing a photograph. It was a bit hard for me to believe that the law school had accepted him. Both Luella and Joan asserted he was indeed a qualified attorney – without a professional job.

As for Joan, she was a woman probably in her middle thirties, with dark-brown hair, sparkling brown eyes, not pretty or feminine-looking, but vigorous, able-bodied, with a deep voice and a hearty laugh. She was greatly concerned with helping black people. She found Paul much more stimulating than any of the white men she had known. I thought that she was an unusual and generous person – as was Paul. But Paul was trapped by the treatment his people had gone through and this made him not exactly bitter, but depressed. Luella would sometimes talk to him softly, or when he was sitting in a chair she would put her hands on his shoulders as if massaging the hurt. I don't know to what extent they were having an affair, but I do know it seemed to me that Joan and Paul were in love and unable to express it, even in private. At a social party in my flat, Paul took the greatest care not to sit near Joan and not to touch me when I was sitting beside him on the floor. I was conscious of his pain.

Much later, back in Canada, I wrote the poem "Remembering New Jersey, 1935." In it I told the true story about a landlady who shouted at me, "Don't ever let a nigger enter my door again!" My reply was, "I never will. Nor a white girl either." I went upstairs to pack.

The director at Memorial House was also an interesting person who was concerned about prejudice against the blacks. She told me that, coming from Canada, I was felt to be less prejudiced. Could I be completely so? Moreover, she was concerned, I suspected, about my politics.

I had in due course submitted my Communist Party card to a committee in the neighbouring town of Hackensack and was accepted to join a cell. In consequence, I had to take the bus, one evening a week, and spend a couple of hours discussing the economic and political scene locally. We were especially concerned about the problems of an Italian working man, a member of the hod carriers' union. I had no idea what a hod carrier was, and did not like to ask. There were also two medical students and an engineer, Ben, in that cell. I can't remember if there were any other women. The medicos were keen to do a tour of the Soviet Union within the coming year. I was envious, knowing that in Canada one would not get permission for such travel. We talked a good deal about theory, the difference between social democracy and communism, but I cannot remember ever participating by demonstrating in the streets or handing out leaflets, as I had done in Montreal. I received a lot of left literature, however, and decided to sign up for a course in Marxist-Leninism at the Workers' School, across the Hudson in New York.

At this time I made the greatest literary discovery of my life. In a Greenwich Village bookshop I found the poetry of Auden, Spender and C. Day Lewis. My one sorrow was that I had no one with whom to share my excitement.

I think that the community house director was concerned mainly about my trips away from Englewood. I did have court cases to attend in Hackensack, but once I stayed overnight without letting her know. What was I really up to? Actually I was combining politics with a new personal relationship. The party member who drove me home once a week was Ben, the engineer, who was a Reformed Jew. It did occur to me that he was an unlikely person to be in a communist cell; the cell embraced such a wide range of people with different economic and educational backgrounds that it bore little resemblance to the organization I had known in Canada. We never saw anyone from the higher echelons, but were handed down decrees: we could not invite a German-American owner of a small building business to become one of us, no matter how sympathetic he seemed to be. Only genuine workers could apply. I looked around and I looked at myself. Only one of us was truly working-class, the Italian-American hod carrier. When his union went on strike, who among us would help on the picket line?

There were all these strands of people around me, sizing me up, as Ben did. After our unit meeting, Ben would give me a ride home to Englewood. Eventually, he became my sleeping partner. I thought of us as being comrades rather than lovers. Nonetheless I enjoyed his slow, undemonstrative companionship. We had no way of meeting socially other than at the party cell, and so we never became really personal or intimate. I began, however, to take it for granted that he was my man.

What a shock I received that night in early January when I had been invited by Ben to what I believed to be a Jewish fundraising dinner. He met me at the bus stop and led me to the hall where there was quite a company of guests. Ben sat me down at the supper table a long way from the head places, where he was gathered with his family. During the serving of the sumptuous meal, short speeches and toasts were made. All in celebration of the engagement between Ben and the young woman beside him! What a trauma I went through, striving not to cry and to look normal. My only solace was the empathy that Scotty showed, reacting to my dilemma.

After that shattering experience, I dropped out of the party. Scotty became my devoted escort. We listened to lectures by his rabbi friend. Sometimes we listened to the opera. Once Scotty invited me to his parents' house for lunch and introduced me as "Dorothy from Canada." Little did I suspect that "Dorothy" was perceived as a Jewish name, and that Scotty's parents regarded me as Jewish and were naturally pleased that their thirty-five-year-old bachelor son now had a girl friend. During this rather one-sided courtship it developed that Scotty intended, with the help of his rabbi friend, to instruct me in the premarital and marriage rituals of Orthodox Jewry. "You mean I am to be converted?" I blurted out, incredulous. "Of course," said Scotty. "I want you for my wife."

"You mean you couldn't tell your parents I'm a Gentile?"

"It wouldn't be necessary," he replied.

"I am much younger than you," I said, "and I do not want to be married. To any man!" Scotty seemed quite baffled; he must really have thought he was saving me from social ostracism.

It must be acknowledged that I owe much to Scotty. It was he who arranged through his carpenters' union to have me take a guided tour through a steel mill in Newark. That tour made a powerful impression on me, although I was unable to create anything from it at the time.

It was true that after a year of working in Englewood I had a sort of nervous breakdown. I felt alien, far from my roots and without any time to meditate or write. So it came about that I resigned from my social work job and returned to Canada in the autumn of 1935.

After several months' convalescence, safe in the snowy woods of Clarkson, I began to revive and relive my New Jersey experiences. First I wrote a long narrative lyric about the farmer's struggle in Ontario, entitled "The Outrider," and, happy with that, I plunged into the documentary poem "Day and Night." E. J. Pratt included the poem in the first issue of his poetry magazine. He was delighted, he said, to find a Canadian poet who was concerned with living people rather than with maple leaves. Remembering Steeltown, I was able to link the speed-up roar of machines with Luella's haunting voice singing spirituals. I wrote a version of a spiritual, included in "Day and Night":

Shadrach, Meshach and Abednego
Turn in the furnace, whirling slow
 Lord, I'm burnin' in the fire
 Lord, I'm steppin' on the coals
 Lord, I'm blacker than my brother
 Blow your breath down here ...

For the same script, I also wrote the ballad, "One step forward, two steps back," using the Marxian phrase in reverse. The background music singing in my head was Cole Porter's "Night and Day." In addition, I wrote a radio play, *The Times Were Different.* It was produced on the CBC and, in 1983, a reading version was presented beautifully at the University of Waterloo, during a conference on my life and work. It is a play about prejudice and how it starts early in a child's education. The hero and eventual mate of the central figure, Margaret, is Jewish. Several of the scenes are based on my experience at Memorial House. Grist to the mill.

It was after regaining my creativity in the spring of 1936 that I received a small legacy from the estate of my aunt, Ina Livesay, the painter in England. That was when I decided to move west, using the newfound funds to stop off in the prairie provinces, giving readings of my own poetry and that of my British contemporaries. This must have been my first poetry reading tour and I loved it. Poetry as oral communication became my goal.

I was headed for a new life on the west coast.

Moving West

I came to British Columbia because I wanted to get to the literary scene in San Francisco. I had been on the editorial board of *New Frontier,* and I was devoted to the magazine and to its aims: namely to document the spirit of the times through reportage, fiction, poetry and literary criticism. The editor, my friend Lon Lawson, suggested that if I went west I could popularize the journal and interview people who might subscribe or write for it across Canada.

My trip by train across the prairies was the best learning experience anyone could have had. I stopped off in Regina and Calgary. With my credentials as a reporter for *NF,* I was able to meet labour leaders who had witnessed the riot of 1935 in Regina when the RCMP attacked a peaceful meeting of the On To Ottawa Trek; leaders of the single unemployed had been explaining their plight to sympathetic people of the city when shots rang out. In Alberta, I talked with the miners of Corbin, on strike for months, then crossed the border into B.C. at Fernie, a ghost company town. The provincial police scanned my identification and believed my story that I was only visiting a relative in that town. Vancouver lay ahead.

It was 1936, one of those west-coast years when April, May and June were sunny all the time. Everyone was out on the beaches or having picnics or attending rallies for the CCF or the unemployed. I felt it was a challenge to stay and see if I could get work. It happened that *New Frontier*'s staff had told me to be sure to look up A. M.

Stephen, a well-known left-wing poet and a member of the Poetry Society in Vancouver. He was also president of the CLDL – the Canadian Labour Defence League, which was an organization for civil rights. Later he became organizer of a United Front group called the League Against War and Fascism.

A.M., as everyone called him, was immediately interested in the magazine I was selling, since its concerns were the same as his: the building of the United Front against war and fascism, and especially for support of the Spanish Republic. I wanted to know about writers, journalists and poets who might like to submit work to us. But also, I needed to find someone who could sell subscriptions. "Well," said A.M., "I think I have just the man for you. He is a Scot from Glasgow – veteran of the Great War who first came to Vancouver around 1920 and fell in love with this young city. He met Dr. Ernest Fewster and other members of the Poetry Society and the theosophical group. Then he went off to Australia. Next we met him returning from China in 1927; and here he is again, having spent the lean thirties in northern Ontario in the gold-mining camps. He is an accountant."

After such an introduction to Duncan Macnair, my curiosity was aroused. It was arranged that we would meet that week on Granville Street near the Birks clock and go to the Honey Dew Café. What I saw was a tall, upright, smiling man in his midthirties, with fine dark hair springing upwards and olive green eyes, who spoke "the Doric," a slight Scottish burr.

"Are you Florence Livesay?" he asked. I burst out laughing, as my mother was well into her middle age; obviously Duncan had never heard of *me*. But he knew and admired, as I did, the poets Charles G. D. Roberts and Bliss Carman, as well as the Toronto poetry lovers associated with them. Wherever Duncan went in his travels around the world he contrived to meet up with poets. That is how he met me.

For me, Duncan's outstanding credential was his enthusiastic response to poets and philosophers. He knew something of politics also, for he had lived and worked in China at the time of its upheavals in the

1920s. He told me at the outset, as we drank an orange drink, that the reason he admired poets like Charlie [G. D. Roberts] was because they toured the inner country, the north and west, meeting Canada's working people. "Poetry should not be shut up in an ivory tower," quoth he.

Well, I could not have agreed more. I showed him copies of *New Frontier* and asked him if he would care to help me sell subscriptions. A.M. would give us a list of contacts. Duncan admitted that since he quit the Ontario mining jobs – from sheer depression at the isolation: "seven years of bondage" – he had been unemployed. He had had a few months as a labourer, digging in the Toronto tunnel, but he yearned for the climate and the spaces of sea and mountain. Any little he could earn would help towards room and board.

Since I had the promise of a social work job with a family welfare agency, it would be possible to meet again at noon hour or after five, with Saturday afternoons free for canvassing. On a bright blue and gold May afternoon we set out to walk to the University of British Columbia, calling on the way on a list of progressive professors. Among them were G. G. Sedgewick, the Shakespeare scholar, Hunter Lewis, A. F. B. Clark and the schoolteacher Madge Portsmouth. We walked all the way to UBC and back, talking our heads off. It was then Duncan told me that his favourite novel was *Diana of the Crossways* by George Meredith. This convinced me that he was a supporter of women's rights and of women artists, just as my father had been. Not that Duncan in any way resembled JFB in appearance or speech, but he was also an iconoclast, a challenger of received opinion. He was ripe for the philosophy that informed *New Frontier* and he was down-and-out, one of the thousands of unemployed single men who were lining up in the soup kitchens of Vancouver's East End. I guess the first gesture I made, as a good comrade, was to invite him for supper at my flat on Haro Street.

We were married in August 1937. Our day would soon be darkened by signs of defeat for the Spanish Republicans, through lack of

D.L. with Duncan Macnair shortly after their marriage in 1937

English and European sanctions against Hitler's tanks and Mussolini's planes.

Our first home was an upstairs apartment on Pendrell Street, a block from the lovely curve of English Bay and backed by the tall cathedral-like forest of Stanley Park. As winter approached I was forced to give up my social work job with the B.C. Welfare Field Service. At that time no married woman could be legally employed in the professions of teaching, nursing or social work. Duncan, however, nearly forty, was eligible for employment as a family man. It was through his left-wing activities and contacts that he acquired an accounting job at Forst's, a Vancouver firm whose management was liberal-minded and progressive. But I grew despondent from lack of work.

Duncan was the breadwinner at twenty dollars a week and I was jobless and without an income. There was no chance of returning to my earlier interest, journalism. Even freelance writing was, for women, restricted to the occasional column on women's topics. "Penny Wise" was the pseudonym of one such columnist.

For five years, from 1932 to 1937, I had been immersed in useful work on behalf of women, the unemployed and peace. Now there seemed no outlet for these interests, and certainly no way of earning "pin money" from writing poetry. I was unemployed. For the second time in my life I became deeply depressed.

By midwinter my association with *New Frontier* magazine as western correspondent began to provide some interest. *New Frontier* was a United Front magazine set up in contradistinction to another, more radically communist magazine, *Masses*. It was to rally the middle-class intellectuals and artists to the cause of the international working class against war and fascism. Lon was editor-in-chief and Gina provided the funds from her capitalist grandfather's estate. Thus, *NF* was not a strictly Communist Party organ; but it was adamantly, to begin with, against the *Canadian Forum's* pallor. J. F. White had been an editor of the *Forum*, but now joined the editorial committee of *NF*, along with Margaret Gould, a social worker; Jocelyn Moore, a librarian; Ross

Parmenter, a newspaper man who had been part of the *Varsity* crowd; Leo Kennedy, and myself. Other assistance came from the PAC, the Progressive Arts Club.

In Vancouver several young supporters rallied to form an editorial committee from the west coast. Leftist journalists – such as Barry Mather, Harold Griffin, Emil and Val Bjarnason, as well as hopeful fiction writers like Bill McConnell, Alice Parsons and the iconoclasts Flare-Pistol Pete Ward and Vernon Van Sickle – met for noon hours at the White Lunch on Granville near Robson, to read their work and to argue where it might be publishable. Generally speaking, the Toronto editorial board turned us down. Even then there was a sense of east-west divisiveness in Canada. We flourished anyway.

There, also, we began to plan how to build a branch of the PAC. Already the PAC had established a workers' theatre in Toronto and Winnipeg. We had envisaged setting up a writers' group, a public speaking group, a drama workshop, a modern dance group and a toddlers' play school. Other creative groups started up with the aid of Harold and Mabel Parker, Elizabeth Keeling, a nursery school enthusiast, and Margaret Carter, an unemployed graduate of the art school. The place, understandably, would be in Vancouver's West End. All that we needed was to find an empty building. The old bathhouse, unused, at English Bay: no sooner had we thought of it than we found a way to reach the parks board. A West End resident, Mrs. Edward Mahon, and a juvenile court judge, Mrs. Laura Jamieson, offered to speak on our behalf. They returned with the news: we could have the bathhouse for a dollar a year! We had a building bee, tearing down the cubicles; merchants of the West End donated materials and in no time the West End Community Centre was born.

I think it was in those rooms that George Goutière, a talented painter of wide interests, taught us the secrets of Stanislavsky method acting.

The real challenge to artists in those days was the unemployed struggle. May 1938 found the jobless single men on a sit-down in the federal post office at the foot of Granville Street, as well as in the city's art gallery. Margaret Carter organized a group from the PAC to draw figures for a mural. In the post office there were young men lying down, standing up, talking, taking sandwiches brought them each day by women sympathizers. After one month the men were met, at 5:00 A.M., June 19, by the RCMP and ousted by means of hoses and tear gas. Their saga for jobs or welfare only ended, for some, when they enlisted in the Mackenzie-Papineau Battalion. Altogether twelve hundred Canadians reached Spain, but only six hundred returned alive.

Perhaps the only written record of those days in Vancouver is the novel by a young woman reporter who followed the jobless to a mass protest in Victoria. Her name was Irene Baird; her novel, *Waste Heritage*. It was and is a fine book. The artists, however, left a more tangible mark: murals by Jack Shadbolt, Charles Comfort and Fraser Wilson. From lowly beginnings the citizens' group that eventually took over the bathhouse was able to carry on its community recreational program right through the war and on into the 1980s. What now exists is a handsome building on Denman Street. On its second floor there hangs a record of the PAC's work: a mural depicting young artists working together at crafts. This was discovered by an old-timer, Harold Parker, who had it lifted from the bathhouse wall, refurbished and cleaned as a tribute to PAC painter and group leader Margaret Carter.

Many were the reasons why I stayed on in Vancouver. The loss of my government job, after marriage, was a depressing blow, but it did give me time for writing and for community volunteer work. Also, at about this time, 1938, I met lifetime friends, Alan and Jean Crawley, who stimulated my literary interests and encouraged me to broaden my perspectives by writing for radio.

The Guide: Virgil

It was in the days at the English Bay bathhouse in Vancouver that the group of mostly young writers stimulated me, but failed to give me what I most needed: serious literary criticism. I had in a sense quelled and submerged any beliefs I might have had concerning the importance of poetry in my life and my own worth as a poet. I was drawn to help create the writers' group at the West End Community Centre, but the acclaim I had been used to in the east, writing documentaries for *Masses* and *New Frontier* and lyrics for the *Canadian Forum,* did not sit well with the preponderantly male members of the group. Poetry was not their main concern. Vernon Van Sickle seemed to be well read in contemporary English criticism, but he had little respect for my views. I was not writing agitprop poetry any more, but ironic political poems along the lines of Auden, Spender and C. Day Lewis. When I read poems such as "English Bay," "Board Meeting" and "Autumn 39," the latter was the only one Vernon approved of. He was known, Duncan told me, to refer to me as "the Duchess." I felt crushed, intimidated. What I most needed was serious literary criticism. Duncan loyally defended me, but he was a nineteenth-century man. What I needed was a lover of contemporary poetry. Alan Crawley was such.

By 1938, Alan and his wife, Jean, had moved to Vancouver from Victoria and were living in the Sylvia Court in an apartment overlooking our bathhouse centre. I learned from poet friends that Alan would like to meet me. They explained that Alan was a Winnipeg corporate lawyer who had been stricken with a virus at the age of 40; he had completely lost his sight. As a diversion he took to memorizing poems that he liked, modern British and American. By the fall of 1934, when the Crawleys moved to Victoria, Alan already had a repertoire of modern poetry that he recited aloud to friends. In January 1935, the ex-lawyer was invited to attend a meeting at the Empress Hotel where modern American poetry was to be recited. At the conclusion, Mr. Crawley rose to his feet. "I cannot see," he remarked in his incisive yet persuasive way, "that the poetry we have just heard is either typically American or typically modern. How about ..." and here he went on to mention the names of contemporary British poets, knowing less, he apologized, of Canadian ones. After the meeting, Doris Fern introduced herself to Alan and asked if he would come to a gathering to meet some local Canadian poets. She mentioned Floris McLaren and Anne Marriott. So it turned out that as soon as Alan met these young Victoria poets he began to make a study of other contemporary Canadians.

In Vancouver, where he moved the following year, he met Anne Angus, who was doing reviews and criticism for the Vancouver press. She was so enchanted by his way of saying poetry that she arranged for readings at the Georgian Club and other Vancouver gatherings.

At the time when we met, that late summer of 1939, my own life was changing. Earlier, in June, I had travelled east to Woodlot to visit my parents. I was in a somewhat rundown state, physically, so it seemed a good time to have a medical checkup. The doctors recommended an appendectomy. Father, ever generous, offered to underwrite the cost of operation and hospital. Some two weeks later I was well and eager to go back to Duncan, who had been writing daily letters of appeal. It was summertime, wasn't it? We should have his one week's holiday together. We could go northwest, explore the coast, board at a camp on Nelson Island, far from the madding crowd. We had never had a honeymoon. We had never gone boating, swimming, fishing. Now was the time to enjoy and to forget politics. Of course I agreed. Once we were there, we decided, in spite of the world crisis, to have a child.

So it was that at the time I met the Crawleys I was already pregnant and anxious to do my stint of good walking. Alan and his spaniel, Roddy, needed a guiding hand. Stanley Park with its seashore and giant firs opened its arms to us. Sometimes, Jean would put Alan on a bus that I would meet, and we would enjoy the whole summer afternoon sitting out under the cherry tree in my backyard until Jean or Michael, their younger son, called by for drinks and social laughter. Often I made notes at night about our conversations, some of which eventually appeared in articles or radio talks.

There was never any lull in our conversation. We talked of politics in Canada, of the Spanish Civil War, of social conditions and of being born in Manitoba, as both of us had been. Alan was greatly interested in my Paris year, when I was studying the French symbolists and their influence on Eliot, the Sitwells, Huxley and Pound.

Alan, who kept a diary at the time, recorded our first meeting and our subsequent friendship:

Later we moved to an apartment on the shores of English Bay near the Macnairs, and as I was once more able to get about a bit, Dorothy often walked with me and my cocker in Stanley Park. We talked of politics, conditions in Canada, social service work, or her youth and mine in the middle west, of the French Symbolists, of Eliot, Auden and Spender, and almost always, of her own writing and what she wanted to do with it. That winter the sense of impending disaster to the world following the warning of the September appeasement was heavy. The Macnairs were distressed at many meetings with men who had returned to Canada after fighting such terrible odds against Fascism in Spain, and they had letters from friends still in that unhappy country. One afternoon, in an unusual sun, broken only occasionally by slashes of wind and rain, we sat together in Stanley Park. I repeated to Dorothy the magnificent "Spain" by W. H. Auden, lately read, that biting indictment of the past and present, and the sombre warning for the future:

"Tomorrow, perhaps the future ....
The stars are dead. The animals will not look.
We are left alone with our day, and the time
    is short, and History to the defeated
May say alas but cannot help nor pardon."

The words sang over and over in our minds. On a nearby bench three men lounged dejectedly, shoulders slouched, heads down and legs outstretched. From time to time one of them got up to throw a stone into the water, and sat down again. Their voices in aimless talk came to us. Evidently they were killing the monotonous hours in idleness. "There," said Dorothy, "there are the men who will have to fight for us when the time comes, the men we will ask to save our country and civilization which has done so little for them. I have seen them in Toronto, in Montreal and now in Vancouver and what am I doing to help them?"

As if in answer to this question, Crawley concluded this part of his reminiscence by describing some poetry readings on the radio that he and I were presenting that spring of 1939:

One evening, after a radio broadcast we read the English translation of "Lament for a Dead Bullfighter," by Lorca, the Spanish poet, and the story of his life, the tragic execution and the burning of his books in Barcelona by Franco's mob. A few days later Dorothy read me her poem, "Lorca."

It took me some courage to read "Lorca," even to such a sympathetic listener as Alan. Writing the poem had excited me because it seemed to come out in a style that was fresh and new for me. I desperately wanted Alan to approve of it. When he told me that he would like to include "Lorca" in all his public readings I was deeply moved.

Although Alan was twenty years older than I, his enthusiasms were those of a boy seeing the world for the first time. And he was blind, for the first time. Even during the dark period of World War II he fought his own battle into serenity. Speaking of his blindness, Alan told me once that the pain was intense for the first year; only when he became totally blind did the pain disappear. I noticed that even in his helplessness his sense of humour never deserted him. "You know, " he said once, "Jean's friends seem to associate blindness with deafness. How they shout at me!" But clearly it was both of the Crawleys' enthusiasm and zest for life that pulled them through.

That was why he was able to respond favourably when I was sent by Floris McLaren and the other women poets in Victoria to ask him to be the editor of a poetry journal. By this time, we were near neighbours: I in North Vancouver, he at Caulfeild in West Vancouver. I took the bus, climbed the rocky steps, was greeted by Jean and offered a cup of tea in the Crawleys' spacious living room. Through the wide window I could watch the Pacific Ocean as it hugged the dark green of Stanley Park. Alan stood up to greet me, offering his hand. As always, he looked directly at me, so there was no feeling that I was talking to a blind man.

Always diffident, modest, he at the same time saw our suggestion as a challenge. Maybe he wasn't an academic or an authority on modern poetry, I told him, "but it is because you are just a lawyer who loves to say poems aloud. You belong to no clique. Your criticisms are impartial. Instead of just giving readings as you have been doing," I said, "we poets desperately need an outlet for our writing, and we need critical reviews of our books. There's nobody west of E. J. Pratt's Toronto-based *Canadian Poetry* magazine!" The year was 1940. Though the McGill group of poets in Montreal had begun to publish, they had not yet produced *First Statement,* edited by John Sutherland, or *Preview*, edited by Patrick Anderson.

Alan could not hide his interest in our west-coast project, but he felt the decision depended entirely upon his wife, Jean. She would have to find the time to read aloud the poetry submissions so that he, as editor, could put them into Braille. Alan asked me for a little time to think and to talk it over, but I felt confident he would take it as a chance to contribute to Canadian poetry as well as occupy his time. In those days no one believed that one could hire a blind man to undertake legal work – or any professional job. "Editor," I assured him, "is right down your alley."

"And what will be the name of this quarterly?" he asked as I rose to leave.

"*Contemporary Verse!*" Already the Victoria group had decided to use this suggestion, which I made remembering an earlier journal printed in the U.S. that I had seen on my mother's desk.

"I like that title," Alan smiled.

A few days later, I was able to telephone the good news to Floris McLaren: "He will do it." It was decided to set up an editorial committee in Victoria with Floris as managing editor, second in command.

From that day forward I was part of Alan's editorial committee, for he usually liked to read selections aloud to a listener before making his final decision. In that way we both discovered new poetry by Earle Birney, Anne Marriott, Jay Macpherson, Miriam Waddington, P. K. Page. There was real excitement in his voice when one day he phoned to say he had spent an afternoon with a remarkable seventeen-year-old from New Westminster, Daryl Hine. Alan was sure he would go far – as indeed he has done, although not in Canada. Alan's inclusion of Daryl Hine's elegant, traditional style alongside Anne Marriott's robust, earthy poem "The Wind Our Enemy" was an example of his eclectic taste. And of course I was very encouraged when he published "Call My People Home." After my thirties documentaries "Day and Night," "The Outrider" and "West Coast," this poem launched me into the forties and fifties.

By the end of the war Earle Birney returned from overseas commitments to a CBC job in Vancouver. It must have been that year that he started a movement for poetry readings in the high schools. He was a prime mover, but he did elicit the help of Alan Crawley, whose readings were already in demand from numerous groups in Vancouver. Alan of course loved having a youthful audience. During that period he was on good terms with Birney. One evening, however, Earle and his wife, Esther, asked to visit the Crawleys to talk about a project Earle had in mind. Duncan and I were invited also. After having drinks, Earle reported that he was now editing *Canadian Poetry* but it was too narrowly centred in Toronto. How much more significant it would be if linked with the west. If *Contemporary Verse* were to become part of this larger project, Birney suggested, it could have a wider readership and better financing and could move from multigraphing to real print.

"You mean," said Alan, his voice quavering, "that I would give up my editorship?" Birney said something about being a western editor. For once I was too shocked to speak. Alan had said all.

I guess this was fair from Earle's point of view. But to the Crawleys and the Macnairs it seemed insensate. What! Just when Alan had made a name for *Contemporary Verse* and had drawn poets from across Canada to write for it and subscribe? Not to mention, as Duncan and I saw it, that the magazine was a great rehabilitative pursuit for a blind man to have.

In any case, that year, in the late forties, Alan declined the proposal. By 1951, however, he himself felt that it was time for the magazine to fold: "It has done its job. There are now *Northern Review* and *Fiddlehead* which have taken up the cause for poetry." I felt crushed, realizing how much I myself owed to the experience of being on the editorial committee, and now dawningly aware that I would see less and less of my dearest friend. I argued with him, of course, but knew it was no use. When Alan made up his mind not even his wife could change him! For me an era closed. Not only Hiroshima but the Korean War dashed all hopes of a peaceful world. Was Auden right after all? "History to the defeated / May say alas but cannot help nor pardon."

In 1970, when Jean Crawley was still alive and Alan was still full of spirited interest in all his literary friendships, he wrote me in Edmonton what I took to be a sort of farewell testimonial. It did not at that time, happily, mean farewell. I quote it only to show the extent of his capacity for generosity and love:

May 3, 1970

I feel confident that you are certain of my affection and the deep gratitude I can never lose for the aid and advice and encouragement that you were so generous with through the years when I was editing. And for the advice and help you have later given to both Jean and me. I feel that I am still carrying too much of the reticent English blood in me to express as I would like to do, the deepest of my feelings.

Although my friendship with Alan Crawley always remained platonic, in the time of my need I was truly in love with this man. He, in his old age, and in his cups, confided that he had also been in love with me. We sustained each other through some dark years, yet remained loyal to our enjoined commitments.

It has been one hundred years and more since Alan Crawley was born in late August 1887. Now, some dozen years since he died, I feel he has never left me. During the last week of his life in the Victoria nursing home, he was not only blind, but deaf. All I could do was squeeze his hand which responded, quick with life. I don't know whether he knew if the bedside person was Dorothy or Pat or Jean, but he uttered stumbling words of love. For in spite of all his handicaps he loved life. I believe he thought of life as a gift, a gift to be grateful for and to make the most of. This view is what I have clung to over my stormy years. Not my father, not my husband, but Alan is the one I think of as Virgil, guiding me always.

Malcolm and Me

The radio voice has been replaced by star wars – Holst's *The Planets*. Mars, god of war. Then Venus, serene queen of peace. Then Saturn, the schizoid. I cannot bear it. Off! But instead of really listening I had been reading four pages of chitchat in the *Province* about Malcolm Lowry. I thought back to my encounter with him that day on the bus to Dollarton soon after the war. I realized that that had been the only time I felt at ease with him, close to him. Here is how I recorded it in a letter I wrote to my friend Anne Campbell:

Today I met Malcolm coming out of Safeway, a Mexican shopping bag under his arm, a blue expression in his blue eyes. He was somewhere, I gathered from the first incoherent answers, in his new book, which is set in B.C. and concerns a lawyer who goes haywire after the case and retires. The book is about his search for a horse, which he keeps losing. Anyway, Malcolm, deep in this, managed to inquire after my family, to say he remembered my poems and how charming it was to be riding on the same bus. He had just come from a North Van beer parlour, where there is all a Dostoyevski needs to know, he says, and why haven't we any serious prose writers? He can't understand it, there is so much to write about in B.C.; there is everything. Well anyway, this blunt, square, almost beseechingly doglike character is writing it. Random House is giving him monthly payments to live on. Just to feel his vibrations convinced me of his genius.

Lowry. The marvellous way he could make words resound with their thousand meanings. He must have lived, in his youth, with a hundred dictionaries, each one providing more and more pathways out of the maze.

And now I remember a Sunday afternoon in our North Vancouver garden when we did talk. In those days after the war, it was most stimulating to be able to share ideas, hear poems and stories being read, discuss the shocking government doings such as the Japanese-Canadian evacuation. I wanted to write about it, but how to find the time to be alone? Malcolm Lowry said to me: "You *must* write. You must forget the children."

"How can I? There's no place to go."

"You could come to our place," he said, including his wife, Margerie, in the offer. "We are taking off for Italy very soon. Wouldn't you like to use our cabin at Dollarton?"

"Right on the beach?" I was enchanted. "I could take the bus for a weekend. But how to get in?" Malcolm arranged for Earle Birney to supply me with the key.

So it happened that one Friday evening in August, with my husband's encouragement, I set off with packsack and pen to write down the experiences I had gone through in interviewing young Japanese-Canadian fishermen torn from their homes after the attack on Pearl Harbor in December 1941.

Ideas were tumbling about in my head on the way to Dollarton. Would this project be a prose documentary or a lyrical, poetic interpretation? I already knew the title: "Call My People Home."

I walked along the forest path down to the beach cabin. In my hand was the key. In the door was the lock. But what good was that key when there had been *another* jailer at work? A spider's web was woven firmly over the lock.

For a moment I felt panic. This was not a good omen. I knew Malcolm had a copy of the Cabala in his library.

"Oh please, please, Lowry the Magician," I whispered, and brushed the web aside. The key fitted. I walked in.

What a relief, just to sit near the wood stove at the oilcloth-covered kitchen table and watch, through the window, small waves curl into the rocks. Or kneel down beside a handmade bookcase. The voices of the young Japanese-Canadian evacuees began to speak to me. I began to write. Much later, after the orange harvest moon had sent its pathway of light shimmering from sky to shore, I took a breath and looked around the tiny two-roomed cabin. Yes, beyond the kitchen area with its narrow couch there was another room – the bedroom, I guessed. Time to put my packsack in place and prepare myself for bed.

As I recall, the door was slightly open. I could see a double bed, some blankets. I lifted my pack and moved to the opening. But what was this? I could not cross the threshold. Something was pushing me back, I knew not what or how. Finally, I threw the bundle in, with a kick. But still I was barred; I could not follow. I returned to the sitting place, the couch. And that is when I remembered what a theosophist friend had told me: "If in danger – psychic danger – say the Lord's Prayer aloud."

"Our Father who are in Heaven ...." I began to say the words.

Revived, but pensive, I stood up and moved to the door lintel. Then I heard my own voice speaking: "Malcolm wanted me to come. I am here. I wish to enter." A deep breath. I entered the room and picked up my pyjamas.

But just in case, I slept on the kitchen couch under the eyes of the moon.

In the morning I wrote a poem:

TALE
for Malcolm Lowry

It was not the lock that disturbed – for I had the key
But over the lock that web of filigree
And the large black witch who watched
From her wheel house, so intricately latched.

Some might have taken warning, gone away
Up sodden path, through evergreen
Past devil's club and spleen
Dashed into daylight and the hard highway.

But I took the key, fitted it into the lock
And turned. The spider house split loose,
Witch scuttled off to hide, fell prey
For the intruder's foot, the stranger's way.
So did I come to own that hen-legged house,
And the house, surprised, grew meeker than a mouse.

Malcolm, I wrote some poems here for you
Defying all black magic: hear me, hold me true.

My final close encounter with Malcolm occurred on the telephone later that same year in wintertime. He knew I was a resource person, a social worker. The Lowrys were living in a near slum on Davie Street in Vancouver, where evictions were taking place. He was concerned about a welfare case, a pregnant mother who had nowhere to go. Although I can't remember the details, it seems that I was able to find an agency that would help her. In response, Malcolm sent me a letter written in pencil:

Dear Dorothy:
It was very good of you to bring some influence immediately to bear, especially when suffering yourself with your hand, of which I'm sorry to hear indeed and hope this may soon be better; as a result of your stretching forth a hand, however, the lady's position is now much less intolerable, she having been teleported to the Newport Hotel. What the Newport Hotel is like I don't like to think, but here it was actively dangerous — the stairs to the attic are so long and steep they make me gasp — indeed her condition was desperate as Margerie immediately saw. Margie had in fact walked half round town and tried about

50 places — literally — before I phoned you, none of which — though many of them run by Catholics, as is this (not to say opposite a convent) which was throwing her out — would take anyone with a baby, far less shortly also to be delivered of another one, even at Christmastime.

It turned out to be fortunate I phoned you though, for the next day she was given an ultimatum by the landlady to get out immediately, whereas previously Friday had been her deadline. Even so there were further difficulties in that she had a brother we hadn't known about and she hadn't owned to (living in a hotel in the skid row apparently) so on and so forth, such being life in this city of terrors: what the brother had to do with it, or even the husband for that matter — who evidently decamped last November — or how in such an appalling pass she could be held accountable for anything whatever I simply don't know. The main thing is that what with you on one end and Margie on the other, something constructive was done ...

Hope the hand isn't too much of a beastly snag with the writing, also to see you soon.

With the best love to your husband and yourself from us both,
   Malcolm

Since those postwar days of contact with the literary life in Vancouver, I saw little of Malcolm Lowry. But I remember that all through those years before his untimely death, Malcolm became a symbol to me of the artist's struggle – regardless of gender – towards independence of thought and action. Even his lapses into alcoholism were a sort of warning to me not to get lost on that track. Moreover, I became interested in the psychic relationship between kindred spirits. My diaries, letters and poems have recorded some of these fascinating serendipities. I am not a Christian and I do not believe in the afterlife. But I believe writers and probably artists of all sorts speak to each other in an unwritten language.

Family Lives

One: A Wartime Marriage

"I will marry you for the coming years, but I cannot promise you that I will stay married when I am fifty. I might want to start another life." How vividly I remember saying that to Duncan before our marriage, August 14, 1937. And now, looking back, how strangely true that prophecy became.

The twenty years between 1938 and 1958 were years of consolidation for me. When war broke out in 1939 we had to give up, or at least lay aside for the future, the idea that our generation could change the world. The fruits of that struggle in the thirties only began to ripen in the seventies; for now, as I write, half the world is socialist or communist. But there was no withering away of the state, as Marx promised; and we must seriously wonder whether the men in charge of the nuclear age are going to destroy our world.

The war and postwar years covered two decades of my life. Marriage, children, housekeeping, nursery school, writing a great deal to earn the little money we were always short of; the record of this is in my articles for the *Toronto Star*, CBC Radio scripts, in two volumes of poetry and two chapbooks.

Day and Night, though published in 1944, contains poems written in the latter years of the thirties. It won the Governor General's medal, an honour only – as in those days no money was attached. Of course there were fewer books of poetry being published, so it was not surprising that I won the award again with *Poems for People* in 1947. This certainly established me as a significant poet in Canada. From then on there were requests to read and speak and teach creative writing. For radio I wrote the documentary drama about the evacuation of the Japanese Canadians from the coast, *Call My People Home*, and after two different CBC performances the Ryerson Press published it in 1952. But another twenty years went by before the Canadian public began to realize what had happened; my play had failed in its aim to rouse the wrath of the people. It was ahead of its time.

Duncan was solidly behind me in all these projects of the forties. From the time of Pearl Harbor, and the crisis caused by evacuation of the Japanese Canadians, my husband was secretary of the Civil Liberties Union in Vancouver. He understood what I was seeking to do in poetry, and as long as I stuck to poetry he was happy.

A veteran of World War I, which he experienced as a youth, Duncan was too restless to return to his birthplace, Glasgow. He literally roamed the world until he settled in Vancouver in 1936, the year I too arrived on the coast. We were deeply attracted to each other, physically and mentally, and we married for love. My father was opposed to Duncan from the start, because he was "shiftless." But he was genuinely unemployed! A single man aged thirty-eight in the Canada of those days had no resources. As soon as Duncan was established as a married man, he got work; then I was forced by law to quit mine. Such was the tenor of the times.

Duncan had been educated not as a Presbyterian Scot but as a free thinker, an admirer of Thomas Huxley and of the Scottish militant labour leaders such as Keir Hardy. He shared George Meredith's liberal view of women and his adherence to theosophy led him to be an advocate of women as creative human beings. All this I was sure of, until there were children, household duties and a very small income. When, after World War II, I sought to remedy the situation to free myself for more writing time, friends laughingly told him, "We know who wears the pants." So Duncan set about taming his shrew, in good

Elizabethan style. A real crisis came when he beat me up and I took the children and ran with them, by bus, to Horseshoe Bay and across Howe Sound to the safety of Roberts Creek. A retired nurse, whom we had dubbed Aunt Ruth because she was a foster mother to difficult or sick children, lived there. Marcie, aged three, had stayed with her for two months with great benefit. Alan Crawley lent me the fare, and it was he who gave Duncan some stringent advice. Our marriage, like most, had its stormy periods. We did love each other. But Duncan was thirteen years older and as time passed he took on the role of adamant father who demanded his comforts. To this I reacted rebelliously, as I had done with my own father. Moreover, our sex life was not happy for either of us. All this was the source of much frustration for us, as many of my dreams and poems reveal. In the poem "Wedlock" I wrote, "We are each one bereft / and weeping inwardly," and "a thousand ancestors have won."

Throughout the forties and fifties, living on the North Shore, we did discover the deep resources of friendship. Jean and Alan Crawley were the greatest support Duncan and I could have had, lacking as we did any older people to help us tussle through the war years with a young family.

The war and having children changed all my perspectives: from being a participant in the struggle for a better world I became an observer. All community efforts narrowed down to that of the home.

Yes, I was still writing poems, time snatched in the basement supervising an old washing machine with hand wringer, or waiting until everyone was asleep to put on a record and write to music. When Peter was born, April 19, 1940, we were renting a rather charming roomy old house on Cumberland Crescent in North Vancouver, overlooking the harbour, where the wartime ships were coming and going. There I wrote the documentary "West Coast." It was published eventually in *First Statement*, but of course I was never paid for it. And we were hard up. Rent was just twenty dollars a month, but Duncan's monthly pay was only one hundred dollars. Fair enough, Duncan would comment, rent should be 20 per cent of income. Then, midwar, our house was put up for sale for two thousand dollars. We had no savings, so could not buy it. We moved twice again before my father helped with a down payment on 848 East 6th Street, North Vancouver.

Throughout these struggling days of World War II, both my parents kept in constant touch with supportive letters and generous gifts. JFB had long given up demanding allegiance to his political views, but FRL was never to deviate or modify her attempt to convert me in religion, politics or daily life. Like many women of her generation, my mother had diminished the demands of her career in order to supervise the household. In 1935 her youngest daughter, my sister, Sophie, had married an Irishman, so she was far away in Belfast. I, however, was near enough to be recipient of weekly news, telephone conversations and arguments.

My political dissensions with my mother had started after my first pull away from the family, that year in Aix-en-Provence. Afterwards, my fourth year at the University of Toronto was crucial. Marxist-Leninism and its dialectic was to influence me for a decade. FRL, on the other hand, became linked with the Ukrainian-Canadian nationalist movement through her work in translating Ukrainian songs and poetry. The concerts she would attend, with gay costumes and dazzling folk dances, could not be acceptable to believers in a communist state. The Ukrainians whom I had come to know in Montreal were still singing, but they were singing the song of struggle: "The Internationale unites the human race." All this was incomprehensible to my mother. FRL still criticized or commented on my writings and still kept her own literary interests, but that was not enough. When it came to personal family relations, she was blocked somehow. She did not ask why her husband was so unpredictable or why her eldest daughter had become such a rebel.

From my marriage onward, FRL continued to try to change everything I believed and did, including the diet I should give my children. I had not become an out-and-out vegetarian, but I was following the new research on diet and health. For FRL this was "a crazy fad." So part of my visits home to Woodlot were marred by our squabbling. Indeed, JFB complained by letter to Sophie in Ireland that the mother-daughter relationship was "fatiguing." Nonetheless, it was thanks to both my parents' support that I was able to take Peter to Toronto where I had registered for a wartime course in day-care and early childhood education. We stayed east for three months.

By the time of our return to Duncan in North Vancouver in April 1942, the attack on Pearl Harbor and the evacuation of the Japanese Canadians from the coast had taken place. I was asked if I would go to the interior of B.C. to be a teacher and social worker for the Japanese Canadians, but my second child, Marcia, was due in July so I had to stay home on the coast. By September's school time I became active in setting up a day-care centre in the North Vancouver Neighbourhood House. Peter was enrolled there. All the experience I had gained in Toronto was put into a program of storytelling, music, painting and play equipment. Peter responded positively, but by the time Marcia was a toddler and we had moved to New Westminster, the wartime tension and anxiety seemed to have become part of her nature. I tried part-time social work, but Marcia became frantic when left with any housekeeper. So I never worked out again, but turned my need for income into writing talks and book reviews for the CBC and articles for the *Province* and the *Toronto Star*.

Two: Parents

In the meantime, way back east, the wartime tensions had had their effect on my parents. The onset of angina and diabetes had led to JFB's resignation as general manager of Canadian Press. This change was a difficult one for him, as he had excelled in this work. He returned to

Woodlot from hospital having to face a life of leisure, an experience he had never met with before. Yet his mind was clear and active as ever, his eyesight keen. He persuaded himself and others that he could contribute to the war effort as he had done in 1917, by writing articles with a Canadian perspective from the front. In high spirits, he set off for London in 1939 or 1940, the year of the phony war. It was not long before he discovered that this was not his war, nor his world. He came back to Woodlot. Here his days were carefully organized: to awake to a cup of tea, have his bath, do his insulin injections, then come downstairs dressed for breakfast. He began to write his book, *Peggy's Cove*. At the time JFB went there, which he did once a year, the cove was a very quiet unobtrusive little fishing village where occasionally artists would come to paint, but there were no photographers and no tourists. I think my father's book became a little classic and may be in part responsible for Peggy's Cove becoming the tourist attraction that it now is. Anyway, JFB was certainly pleased to have written the book and supplied the photographs that accompanied the text.

My last visit to Woodlot occurred well after the full-blown war was in progress. Early in 1944, JFB and FRL, in harness, had come through a cold, snowy winter isolated in the woods except for a gardener-chauffeur and a daytime housekeeper. Now, in May, spring had arrived with its delights: daffodils and trilliums scattered through the woodland valley. Woodlot was in its prime, every detail of its Geor-gian architecture brought to fruition as JFB had planned it. Visitors were welcomed to see the flowers. Indoors, the radio was at hand with its promises of peace. There was indeed a feeling in the air that the iron clutch of war was weakening, that this would be its final year. As a result, our family communication improved. JFB and FRL wrote suggesting that they would like to see Marcia, two-and-a-half, for the first time, and Peter as a four-year-old. Letters bounced back and forth. At first Duncan did not object, but he must have felt pretty lonely. He was by that time employed as an accountant at a lumber mill in New Westminster, so we could sublet our house and he could board in

Burnaby with my aunt, Helen Randal, a B.C. nursing inspector and editor of *Canadian Nurse*. Let us say that concerning my trip east with the children, Duncan acquiesced under pressure. Lack of money had been the bane of our marriage, and often JFB had helped. I felt it was now my turn to bring some pleasure to my parents.

It was rather fun on the train going east. There were plenty of young soldiers aboard, and cheerful black porters who kept their eyes on the moral behaviour of young girls. Peter electrified the passengers when the train stopped at Regina by shouting, "Mummy! It rhymes with vagina!" Marcie was shy, but attracted attention because she was a little golden-haired butterfly running up and down the aisles. When we arrived in Toronto, Father sat out in the parked car and Mother, in the station, opened her arms as Marcie ran towards her never-seen-before grandmother. The drive to Clarkson and Woodlot revealed the countryside, at end of May, beginning to be green and lilac-filled.

How I specially like to remember my father taking little Peter for walks through the spring woods. Once they saw a garter snake and my father reached down and picked it up. He let his grandson touch it. "You see," he said, "it can't hurt you." Marcia, unlike everyone else in the Livesay family, had brown eyes, but fair skin and golden hair. JFB would hold her on his lap to share his late breakfast toast and marmalade. "She's going to be a beauty," he told me. It turned out that she was not always compliant, for an area of the garden that he had fenced in for a safe play yard was utterly rejected by his little granddaughter. Peter had no interest in climbing in beside her to keep her company. Grandfather surveyed the abandoned cage and said, ruefully, "I guess I'll have to get chickens."

By mid-June the irises were in full glory, their doggy faces each differently coloured in purple, bronze or gold. On June 14, the family – consisting of FRL, Peter, Marcie and myself – had been out for a country drive with JFB at the wheel. On our return to Woodlot in late afternoon we followed FRL to the front door and there, tucked around the doorknob, was one solitary iris bloom.

"Look, Live!" FRL said, with meaningful intonation. "Why, yes," he replied, taking the flower into his hand. "Someone has called. Perhaps Anne?" He strode through the doorway, as usual, always ahead of the family. After tea, he remarked that this was his day to remember Mary Harris's birthday. So he looked for his shears in the kitchen drawer and went out into the garden to cut a bouquet for his longtime friend.

Now alone with the children, I remembered the story of JFB's arrival in Canada, and especially his arrival into that part of Ontario that is now called Mississauga. The young immigrant had relatives in Cooksville, the Gordons, and connections in Erindale and Clarkson. Of these, the Harrises, who lived as gentlemen farmers in their colonial homestead, Benares, had been his closest friends. Mary Harris had reminded JFB of his mother, the Plymouth sister, Sophy Bligh Livesay, and Mary's eldest daughter, Anne Harris, became JFB's first sweet-heart.

What had happened to that budding love affair?

Because young Fred Livesay was jobless and penniless, the Harris family council ruled that a marriage would be out of the question. He must go west, go harvesting. He went, but only to return again, time after time, and eventually to buy nine acres from the Harrises' property. Meanwhile Anne had married, borne children and divorced. She lived now in a log bungalow just across the ravine from Woodlot. Yes, I thought, it must have been Anne who called at our door that day.

At dinnertime I summoned up my courage to say that we would soon be leaving for the west. "I've booked the berth," I told my parents. FRL looked relieved. "I guess it's time," she smiled. JFB said nothing.

Later that same evening, after putting the children to bed, I came downstairs to see my father sitting in his armchair as usual with a pack of cards and his cribbage board. JFB had always said, and I agreed, that I did not possess a card mind. Yet, cribbage being a relatively simple game, he tolerated my partnership. His wife had never played cards, so I knew that during the long winter evenings that lay ahead he would be playing solitaire. Now, in hot, muggy summer weather, we played three games intensely. For the first time in weeks, I won. I was cheered, yet puzzled. Was he just letting me win? Or was he losing his grip? He looked tired.

Next morning, June 15, I was awakened around eight o'clock to hear my mother calling from the next bedroom. "Dorothy! Dorothy! Come quick! I think something has happened." I stumbled along the hall and found her in JFB's bedroom. He was lying there motionless, his mouth slightly open, his eyes closed. "Is it –? Is he –?" she begged me. I went up to the bed, touched his hand and picked it up. It still seemed to be warm, yet there was no pulse. The shock was incredible. I had known that my visit was ending and that I would be going back to Vancouver in a week's time, but I was stunned. I was hardly aware of what was happening.

"He's dead," I said dully. Then, "Phone the doctor." FRL said it was strange that he had not called out, as he usually did with an angina attack. "And look, he's been taking his nitroglycerin! I just had it filled!" The bottle was empty. "Call the doctor," I repeated. But when Dr. Vernon came, FRL told him she wanted no autopsy. This led me to imagine that perhaps JFB had committed suicide. Now, however, I know that nitroglycerin, no matter how much is ingested, cannot be fatal.

FRL phoned Harry Day of the Canadian Press and from then on he and she took charge of all arrangements: funeral, news coverage and the will. She behaved with almost no sense of having any feelings. I couldn't communicate with her at all. But I knew my mother was particularly flustered because for two or three days she and Mr. Day could not find the key to the filing cabinet that contained all my father's private papers. According to the will, all these papers were to be sent to I. Norman Smith, publisher of the Ottawa *Journal*. But, obviously, FRL did have access to the cabinet and its contents, once the lock was broken.

The three days before the funeral were a kind of nightmare. I couldn't sleep. The housekeeper came and gave me brandy. Somehow we sent the children to friends to be looked after so that I was able to join in the funeral. The old gardener, who had been very close to my father, had neglected to clean our car; this upset my mother, of course, very much. The service was attended by many newspaper men and family friends. It was the kind of service my father would have liked, held in St. Peter's Church, Erindale. Though my father never went to church, the parson had been a good friend of his. The first hymn to be sung was his childhood favourite, "Onward Christian Soldiers." Then the Canadian Press staff carried the coffin out into the cemetery and planted it, as he had requested, under a spreading oak tree.

When we arrived back in Vancouver by train, Duncan was full of sympathy and tenderness. We had to stay in a friend's house for a while until our new abode was available. I remember being happy with my husband's solicitude and hugs. In the middle of that first night back I awoke with a line running through my head. The result was the poem "Inheritance."

In the rooms of my mind you pace
Sad parent, your own head thorned —
Not in my power to bestow or bless
No gesture for surcease.

Some silence there was: sun's fierce
Assertion on a windy height,
Some daylight peace. But none to pierce
Shouting abyss, and raving night.

They called you shy; a blusterer —
Two poles, stretched agony between
And some might wonder why the grass grew green
Where acid words had lately been.

In the rooms of my heart you race
Fiery father of us, your kind
Your burdened brood; who yet will face
The day, the dark; housed in a quiet mind.

For at least a year after his death I would dream about my father. One dream I remember vividly was one in which we were driving – him beside me. I can't remember if he was on my right and I was driving or whether he was driving and I was on his right. But he was almost a skeleton and he said, "Ha! There's life in the old boy yet!" I realized it would take me a long time to recover from my father's influence.

My regret now about those last visits I made during the forties, the war years, is that although I afforded my father quite a bit of companionship and he enjoyed his grandchildren, we never really became intimate or spoke of our mutual problems in marriage. I took it very much for granted that my parents would pay my way to Toronto and give me room and board with Peter and Marcie. They put up with the problems of having two toddlers in their house, so full of precious objets d'art.

JFB did not live to see my award-winning book, *Day and Night,* nor indeed the publication of his own *Peggy's Cove.* He never had to face Hiroshima or the drastic changes in the postwar world.

Three: A Postwar World

A year or so after my father's death I did receive a kind of message from him. I had a dream in which JFB told me to write to Mr. Hindmarsh of the *Toronto Star,* for whom I had worked in the thirties. The message was: *Offer to go to England to describe the postwar rehabilitation in progress.* To my considerable astonishment and apprehension, a telegram came back forthwith, offering me two or three months in England, my fare there and back, and very good pay on the basis of three articles a week.

This was my first real opportunity to go it alone, although I had been east with small Peter during the war. But this time I would have to leave the children and arrange for their care. Today, I wonder how I managed it. My only close family relative in Canada was my mother, and she agreed to come from Toronto to stay in our New Westminster home, apparently without any qualms. Neither she nor Duncan realized that she wasn't resilient enough to cope with small children. I knew she couldn't keep house or cook to any extent, but a cleaning woman would be assisting her. By October 1946, FRL was installed and I was on my way, flying to London.

About two weeks later, Duncan threw in the sponge and told his mother-in-law to leave. He sent the children to boarding care in the country at Roberts Creek. Peter was six, just starting school. Marcia, in particular, flourished in the quiet, relaxed and loving atmosphere of "Aunt Ruth's." When I returned home some two months later, our family was most happily reunited.

But while I was away I had had enough experiences to give me a new lease on life, new vistas. As it happened, a very good friend was back in London from British Columbia, where she and two children had been refugees. She was Celia Strachey, wife of John Strachey, the journalist. He was now minister of food in the British postwar government. I was happy to be invited for a weekend at their country home, with time to walk and talk with the minister. One of our stops was at the village store, where John collected his family ration of oranges – golden oranges from Greece, no doubt. I could see that this detail would make a neat headline for the *Toronto Star*. My meeting with Strachey also led to introductions to the planners of new-style housing developments and new school programs.

Hindmarsh must have approved of all this, for instead of beckoning me back to Canada he sent me to Ruhr, to do a survey of rehabilitation programs in areas of Cologne and Düsseldorf. I was put up at the

D.L. posing for a newspaper photographer, 1950

British military press camp and given a chauffeur who spoke some English. I had to recall my high-school German, but actually two important people whom I interviewed in West Germany were comfortable with English. One was a hospital doctor, the other a professor of English in Cologne. And there were schoolteachers who had hidden the *Jalna* novels under their skirts.

By the time I returned to Canada I had enough material to write the novella *Give My Love to London*, which was never published, and poems for the book *Poems for People*. I continued to write articles on social and living conditions, this time about B.C., for the *Star* and the *Star Weekly*. I was also given a generous helping hand by CBC Radio in Vancouver. They produced *Momatcum*, a poetic documentary on the plight of B.C. native people. A few years later, in 1952, the same people produced *Call My People Home*.

After my father's death I had natural concerns about how my mother would manage. FRL was in perfect health and displayed unflagging interest in her ongoing projects: translating Ukrainian folk literature and studying the genealogy concerning her own family, the Randals and the Andrews. In addition, she researched the Livesay family tree in England.

I cite this aspect of my mother's widowhood simply to show how she was able to throw herself into new interests. Although often unlucky and beset by failures, she remained plucky. This trait related also to her business dealings. She had never had any knowledge of marketing or real estate, but she proceeded to sell Woodlot and to buy a small house in Toronto on Delisle Street. This would have been about 1946. She took along her large library of Canadiana, storing it in an empty garage – only to have it flooded during a thunderstorm. Thereafter, with the help of Gil Purcell at the Canadian Press, she sold that bungalow in exchange for one in West York. It was there that I stayed, with Marcie, for a month one summer when I was doing a part-time project at the Infant's Home. Grannie delighted in taking bus trips with Marcie, going as far as Niagara Falls. She was pleased that I did the shopping and cooking and that she would have "someone in the house at night."

When I returned to Vancouver, FRL began to let a room to a series of male boarders. Finding this unsatisfactory, probably to both parties, she sold the house and began looking for one closer to her roots in Clarkson. She found a place in the town of Grimsby, where she had friendly connections with the Anglican Church and with an artist friend of my sister Sophie's, Helen Brown. Much to the amusement of these friends, FRL arrived at the Grimsby house sitting in the front seat of the moving van, alongside an old steamer trunk, filled – of course – with papers. In the back were more and more boxes of Canadian books. And she would be eighty that November of 1953, happy and busy as ever. By this time, FRL had translated and scripted a classic Ukrainian poetic drama, *Song of the Forest*, written by a woman poet. The script, she thought, would be "beautifully suited for television." So one July day, she arranged to visit Toronto by bus to talk with a CBC TV editor. She would be staying overnight with a dear long-time literary friend, Mrs. Valance Patriarche.

During that same week, I was holidaying with Peter and Marcie in Kelowna. Every year we used to rent a cottage for the month of July, ending with Duncan's two-week vacation. So I was alone with the children when, on a Sunday, a phone call came from my Aunt Helen in Burnaby. She told me that the Canadian Press had advised, "Mrs. Livesay seriously injured in a bus accident. Now in hospital." I asked my aunt what I should do. Her reply: "I advise you to fly east at once." It was Sunday morning and I knew there was no air service from Kelowna. On the telephone I talked it over with Duncan. I would have to take a train to Calgary and from there fly to Toronto. What, I wondered, should I do about the children, aged thirteen and eleven? My uncle, Phil Randal, offered to put them on the evening train to Vancouver, where their father would meet them.

I flew, just after midnight, from Calgary to Toronto. Now I was alone. If only I could reach my mother in time! But it was not to be.

On arrival, at about seven in the morning, I called the Toronto General, only to hear the words, "She passed away at midnight." Had I failed her again, or had she understood?

My next efforts were to contact Mrs. Patriarche who, when FRL never arrived, began phoning hospitals and police. It seemed that my mother was standing in the aisle of the bus when it stopped very suddenly. She was thrown against the steering wheel and ruptured her spleen. Later, I contacted her favourite nephew, Alan Randal, who himself had been employed by the Canadian Press. He was in Toronto at the time and was with FRL on her last day. Alan told me it was good I did not see her, as she looked terrible. Nonetheless, she was perfectly conscious. "Don't trouble Dorothy," she had told him. But when they did contact me, it was too late.

After the funeral at Erindale Church, where my mother was buried beside her maverick man, Live, Alan drove me to the home in Grimsby to see what needed to be done with all the belongings. We decided I would have to stay on for a few days, especially to sort through the papers in the steamer trunk. I have never felt more alone than during those days, selecting papers and letters to be kept and burning others outside in the brick barbecue. That evening a huge wind came up and blew the blackened scraps of paper, ragged crow's wings, all over the yard and even into the neighbour's yard. I felt quite frightened at the idea of sleeping in my mother's bed. I kept the radio turned on beside me. But finally, in the morning as I was waking, I felt my mother to be very close at hand. She was saying, "It will be all right. It will be all right, dear girl." From that day on, my burden of guilt was lifted.

My mother's diaries were left in my care. It was only as I read the entries from 1902 to 1908 that I came to know that she had been, in her own way, a feminist. A feminist, but sadly restricted.

During the mid-1970s, when I was writer-in-residence at the University of Manitoba, a woman came into my office. She was doing her Ph.D. in Slavic literature, using my mother's translations as a basis.

I was delighted at the idea and offered to let her see the documents I had deposited at the Museum of Man, now the National Museum of Civilization, in Ottawa. The end result was a beautiful coffee-table book, *Down Singing Centuries*.

It was after I had delved long into those unblackened papers that I began writing poems about my mother and her marriage, which I had such trouble understanding as a young and questioning girl. Here is the one poem that is, perhaps, the closest to the truth:

The Origin of the Family

Where my parents canoed
on the Red River
on Sunday afternoons
before coitus
before I was conceived

the river flows on
seventy years after
without a trace
of his paddle's grace
or her low laughter

It's all in my head
their conversation
their efforts at
conciliation —
the nagging question:
are we in love
or not?

Because, at long last
September 1, 1908
they went to church, took the train
to Whytewold on the lake
to a borrowed honeymoon cottage
mice scuttling over their faces
and in the morning
he cooked the eggs and bacon
he swearing like a trooper
("I'd never heard him swear before –
and I've never got used to it")

Was it because
he had decided she wasn't a virgin?
She never knew till twenty years later
why he resented her body and her ways
and how she had no chance
ever to prove to him
her essential innocence …

Four: New Directions

By the early fifties I began to see that I would have to plan for a life of my own after the children were educated. I had so much enjoyed teaching creative writing at UBC's Extension Department, and then working at the YMCA for two years as a young adult supervisor, that I decided I would like to qualify as an adult education teacher. Unfortunately, there were no such courses at UBC. Instead, the education faculty advised that I would have to enroll for a year's course to get a high-school teaching diploma.

I quail now as I think what this meant for me, physically and emotionally, and what it meant by way of change for Duncan and family. Today, many young married women pursue such courses without a qualm, but I was considered quite mad for doing so, especially by my husband's Scottish friends. It was, I can see, a considerable upheaval for Duncan to put our New Westminster house up for rent and live in a small wartime "hut" at Acadia Camp, UBC. It was irksome that the bedrooms were small. Marcia and I each had our own, while Peter and Duncan had cots in the third. Only a thin wall separated us from our neighbours. I had to use my room as a study area, preparing not only papers for my education course but also lectures for the first-year English students at UBC. It was only because the head of the department of English gave me a first-year section to instruct that we were able to make this move a financial possibility. Duncan had to commute by bus from the university to his new office job downtown. But there was a compensation: the university social life. Our close contacts were with Geoff and Margaret Andrew. They had children who were the same ages as ours and were attending the same progressive and lively school, University Hill. Peter flourished, whereas Marcia found it hard to adjust, as was the case whenever we had to move to a new environment – even for summer holidays.

I kept up my contacts with poets and with CBC people and, that year, Jay Macpherson published my small chapbook, *New Poems*, my first book since publication of *Call My People Home*. In general, the political and cultural life in Canada was at a low ebb. George Woodcock had yet to put his hand in and found the literary quarterly *Canadian Literature*, and the Canada Council did not yet exist. The Korean War dampened all our spirits.

When we moved to North Vancouver from UBC in the summer of 1956, it was to a new house on Grand Boulevard. We had bought this at quite a risk, as houses were scarce and house prices were soaring. But I had the assurance of a teaching position at Magee High School in Vancouver. I would be near the bus to town and the children would

D.L., 1950

be only a block away from Sutherland Junior High. Duncan's job as accountant at Denby Brothers was shaky, but he got into something he liked much better, as accountant for the Grouse Mountain ski lift and resort. We all liked the modern bungalow facing the park on Grand Boulevard, and the mountains beyond. It seemed that all would be well. Alas, I put in two of the worst years of my life, trying to teach teenagers. I had loved teaching adults and had, I think, a good rapport, especially with women. At university, my freshman class was a bit dicey because there was a great wave of listlessness and lack of ambition prevalent. I succeeded, however, in encouraging two or three young men and that was as much as I could expect, being more of a writer than a teacher, more of a permissive mother than a rigid disciplinarian. The iron hand, I learned to my deep grief, was the only way to handle high-school students, even in grade twelve. The next year, the board of education of Vancouver gave me one more chance to qualify for a permanent certificate, giving me a grade-eight class at Point Grey Junior High, with grade-ten French and a girls' class of HPD, Health and Personal Development. To begin with, that spread was far more than I could handle, physically. If I had been given one grade-eight class in a poor area of the city, I think I could have made it – and been happy at it. Instead, I was in a wealthy, upper middle-class area where the children really had no respect for adults. The teachers who got grudging respect were those whom the students feared.

Help did come my way, however. I was advised to resign from the school board that spring of 1958, presumably instead of being fired, and I applied for a new grant that was being made available by the Humanities Council for teachers who would like a refresher year in a country where they could observe and study their own discipline. I knew from educational reading that the British method of teaching English as a creative subject was greatly to be preferred to the rigid and old-fashioned British Columbia program. So I applied for the bursary and I was awarded a grant of $2000, through the intervention of a poet friend, Dr. Roy Daniells of the English department at UBC. My joy may be surmised, and also the complications that this offer presented.

How to persuade Duncan to let me leave the family for six months? Several factors helped. Our great friends, the Crawleys, urged him to "let Dorothy have her fling" because the children were now old enough to be on their own. Peter had finished high school and was going to take a year working at a job before going to university. He had worked every summer at forestry and fishing, and now he had an offer to be with a land survey crew. Marcia had a scholarship to become a boarder at a boys' and girls' progressive school near Aspen, Colorado. Duncan had not wanted his daughter to accept, but she was nearly sixteen and told him it was her chance to avoid going to North Vancouver High, a deadly place as Peter had found. She wanted to go south.

All these plans would leave Duncan entirely alone, for the first time in his married life. But he had roamed the world until he was thirty-eight! He was sixty-one, but looked much younger, with the same old vigour for mountain climbing. On the other hand, there was an economic consideration: in four years he would be retired and receiving only the government old age pension, as he had steadfastly refused to take out life or job insurance; in those days there was no bonus such as the Canada Pension. So I would certainly have to be working. Duncan was intelligent enough to know all this; but he must have been emotionally torn to see old age approaching and the family taking off. Yet, Duncan seemed hale and hearty; I think none of us, family or friends, ever thought of him as aging. He had always had a remarkably strong constitution, one of the few World War I veterans who never required medical aid or hospitalization throughout his life.

The decision was made by both of us that Duncan would stay on in our house facing the park on Grand Boulevard, with our devoted Scottie dog, Sukey. A young couple we knew, presented with their first baby, were desperate to find a place to live; they agreed to board Duncan and look after the housekeeping. And so it was, with scarcely any forebodings, and no regrets, that I set off on my first real march towards freedom. It was September 1958. Ahead lay the third year of my life in which I could live abroad.

Five: Going It Alone

It was a breathless time, that autumn. I had not only to find a place to live, but also to get accepted in a seminar course led by James Britton at the University of London Institute of Education. After a trial rooming house behind Trafalgar Square, I moved closer to the university at the Penn Club, a Quaker boarding house on Bedford.

Although members of the Penn Club were presumably devotees of peace who attended meetings of Bertrand Russell's Ban the Bomb movement, as I did myself, I did not strike up more than a casual acquaintance while living there. My solitary bacon-and-egg breakfasts, my lone table at the heavy noonday dinner, made me feel like an intruder, only in England on sufferance.

There was one boarder from the top floor who aroused my curiosity. He was a stocky, red-nosed, middle-aged Englishman named, I was told, John Harris. He stayed upstairs every day, just writing. One of the students told me, sotto voce, that he was a famous novelist, a writer of science fiction. He wrote under the pseudonym of John Wyndham. One day, arriving home after a morning as observer in a Quaker high school, I was surprised to find a fire engine in front of the tall London row house. Against one side was a long ladder reaching to the top floor. Two firemen seemed to be scaling it.

"But where is the fire?" I asked a bystander.

Nobody knew. Inside the dining room there was no sign of smoke or panic. A young man finally volunteered enlightenment: "That's John's latest novel. A crime has been committed in an attic room."

"You mean he hired the fire department?"

"It would appear so."

I decided, on my long underground trips to schools, to start reading a novel by John Wyndham.

My seminar took place one evening a week, beamed over by James Britton, that delightful teacher whose passions were poetry and poetry in the schools. There was only one other Canadian graduate in the group. The English person I was most drawn to was a youngish poet and public school teacher named Alistair. We had fiery exchanges in class and closer flashes of laughing intimacy after class, as we walked to his Tottenham Court Road tube station. It seemed that Alistair lived with his wife and family many miles away and was always afraid of missing the last train south. Did we correspond between sessions? I do not remember. But when I wrote a series of London poems, one wintry poem, "A Ballet of Squares," was written for Alistair.

Another friend I had was a nephew of Charles G. D. Roberts's, Goodrich Macdonald. He was a rather shaky old man living near Soho. He had made it his business to get to know the cellar clubs where poets such as Dylan Thomas and writers like Anthony Burgess congregated.

My encounter with Anthony Burgess was quite a surprise. He and his wife had returned to England from Malaysia and often went pubbing in Soho. During an entire evening in a bar he told me the story of his supposedly fatal brain tumour. "They gave me no more than a year to live and sent me home to die. But here I am after a year, alive still, and intending to stay so." Somehow I felt immensely cheered. That British stubbornness was an admirable quality. Tenacity. Both my parents had possessed it.

The London stimulus was such that I felt as young as if I were just a graduate student returning for a year's refresher course. More importantly, I was enjoying the freedom to speak out on the subject so dear to my heart, teaching creative English, and with a chance to sit in on different school classes at every level of British education. I wrote a long monograph on this subject for publication in B.C., but it was never printed in its entirety because no magazines existed that would print it in Canada. Also of special significance for my future was another workshop I attended as an auditor: "On Teaching English as a Second Language." At the same time I was corresponding with Duncan in North Vancouver, and Marcia in Colorado, letter upon letter. I was also writing to Alan Crawley, whose replies I rejoiced in. At this time, I was writing poems about the London gloom: "Mothering Sunday," "Cyprus," "The Dismembered Poem."

And where was that Christmas spent? In Paris? Belfast, with my sister? I only remember being back in London by January and February, again attending the institute classes and visiting schools. On a Friday afternoon in February I went to a university concert where *Dido and Aeneas* was being performed, an opera I had never heard before. It took my breath away. As I walked to the Penn Club in the gathering dusk my mind was still harmonizing, tethered to that music of Purcell's in which Dido dies and Aeneas goes off to found Rome.

In the narrow hallway of the club was a rack for letters and a bulletin board. I barely glanced there when I noticed a thin blue envelope with my name on it. Tearing it open, I read, "Father passed away last night, February 12. Love, Peter."

I stood in the hall, shaking. Instead of going upstairs to my room, I went outside again, stumbling along into the twilight street. The only words that would come to me were, "I'm free ... I'm free ..."

On my return to the house, I met the club secretary, brusque and British. "When did this telegram come?" I asked her. "Oh, around noon," was the response.

"My husband has died," I told her.

"Indeed!" she replied. Nothing more.

That's when I came to my senses and telephoned family friend Gwladys Downes, who was then studying in London. From her flat we spent several hours trying to get through to North Vancouver by telephone. Finally, there was an answer from Jimmy Campbell, a close family friend; he gave me the details. A massive stroke. Duncan had been taken to emergency in a coma. Peter was with him throughout the night. My son was arranging for the funeral and wanted to know when I would be coming home.

It took another two or three hours that night before I could confirm a flight to Vancouver. Marcia had to fly home also, from Colorado. The memorial service was held at the Vancouver Unitarian Church, where a passage was read from Duncan's favourite essayist, Edward

Carpenter – a recluse, a gentle theosophical essayist – and from Dylan Thomas's wonderful elegy for his father, "Do not go gentle into that good night." As he would have wished it, Duncan the theosophist was cremated. His close friend, Arthur Peacey, and our son, Peter, aged eighteen, were my strong supports.

In one week's time we sold the house on Grand Boulevard. I flew back, into the arms of London. There, at the end of 1959, I was heading for my fiftieth birthday. What lay ahead was a new life in Paris, with UNESCO. Then Lusaka.

I had worn four hoods: childhood, girlhood, womanhood and motherhood. Now there were two more waiting: widowhood and selfhood.

La Vita Nuova

Could I have left it there, my life? That May and June in London, 1959, I began to feel loss and guilt regarding Duncan's death. Had I stayed at home in North Vancouver would he have had that fatal attack? This mystery I will carry along with me, ever after, as well as the mysteries of my mother's six-month silence before her wedding, my father's death, Knister's drowning and Gina's sudden going. What shapes the truth, I wonder. And is it always seen "through a glass, darkly"?

Nonetheless, a new start had to be made. I had no thought of aging, of dying. I had predicted that at age fifty I might want to be done with marriage, done with family care or free-lance jobs. I wanted a taste of professional life, financial security; above all, I longed to experience the lot of young people in the third world, a world headed for independence from colonial domination. Ghana achieved that status first. Then Nigeria. That June of 1959 my family was permanently scattered. Peter was at UBC headed for anthropology as a career; Marcia had been accepted at Queen's University, Belfast, and was to live there for three years with Sophie. I wrote to my former professor of French, Felix Walter, who was then the head of the French education section of UNESCO in Paris. How could I get a job, I asked him, as a teacher of English in India or Africa? He was most encouraging: Come to Paris and we'll talk it over, he wrote me.

I did just that. And learned the best way to reach my goal would be to live in Paris, working at UNESCO as a temporary researcher in educational problems. Indeed, eventually there came an opening in the section concerned with the education of girls and women. No need to say anything further: I was overjoyed. I spent the summer months doing office work in the UNESCO building and then was appointed to three months in the section dealing with girls' education, worldwide. This department was doing a survey. It had sent out a questionnaire via the nongovernmental organization of UNESCO. I was to appraise the statistical results, for a report entitled "Women's Access to Post Secondary Education." I worked under the supervision of a specialist, a French-speaking expert who in turn communicated with her supervisor, a Russian. This elderly lady spoke no English and only very little French. Difficult though my relationship with these women was, I hung on because I was able to know first-hand where the requests were coming from for UNESCO field appointments. I applied to go to Northern Rhodesia. By November I was accepted and ready to go.

All I could see, squinting through the plane's wing window, were humps and clumps of soft furry brown – hills and trees braced and bent together. Above them the sky seemed shriekingly blue. It was November, towards the end of the dry season. The plane's descent to Lusaka airport reminded me of landing in Manitoba on a day of early spring: grass withered, leaves strewn in brown paper curls. Space everywhere. Deep silence, except for the teasing wind.

I was duly met by a chauffeured car and an education officer of the Federation of Rhodesia and Nyasaland. What is now Zambia was then the third province of the federation, the government of which was in Salisbury. So Lusaka wouldn't be much of a city, I thought, just a provincial seat. The drive through burnt brown fields and past the African village or "compound," with its shacklike dwellings and aluminum roofs glinting in the sun, scarcely prepared me for a wide city boulevard, startlingly colourful, with the blossoming trees whose names I had to begin to learn: violet jacarandas, flaming flamboyants, poinsettias trembling in the wind. Behind them rose the graceful white columns of modern office buildings. And in the shade of the acacias black men in white shirts were talking and gesticulating, standing or squatting, selling their wares. In sharp contrast were the women with red bandannas and long rainbow-coloured skirts, many with a baby hammocked on the back.

Children were everywhere, barefooted, small, sometimes ragged. Since the African Education schools – separate from those of the coloureds and the Europeans – were on both a double shift and a year-round rotary system, there were always children on holiday, playing or lounging on the boulevards.

There were no buses, I learned. Africans walked. Europeans drove. Africans were called Bantu. Anyone with white skin was simply European: my Canadian identity gone after half a century in Canada.

Little did I know then how close we were to a breakup of Sir Roland Welensky's federation. Indeed, my view of the whole country was to be narrowed down to what went on in one small community, a teacher-training college on the outskirts of a mining town, Kitwe, in the centre of the Copperbelt.

Kitwe Training College was two miles or so outside the town along a red sand road, soon to be paved. Driven in a Land Rover, I arrived one day in November at the college. It was past noon. No one was in sight or earshot. I went to the principal's office and then set out for the dining hall. A teacher in white shorts ran after me, redirecting the Land Rover to the principal's house, a pleasant red brick bungalow set in a residential row behind the school buildings.

Mr. B., a small wiry man with a kindly north-country voice, brought me to meet his wife and four children. We sat down almost immediately to dinner. Without any preliminaries he told me that he had not expected me for two months and the week before he had called the superintendent in Lusaka about my assignment: "Should I treat her gently and let her observe – or should I make her one of us?" Mr. Little, the superintendent, had insisted I should be treated just as one of the staff. I told the principal quite frankly that I had had different instructions from UNESCO headquarters.

But obviously, I added, now that I was on the spot UNESCO could not make decisions for me. So I would like some time to observe the classes.

"Easy enough," he said. "You've got three weeks before the college term ends at Christmas. During that time we'll have to fix you up with a house, a houseboy and a car."

The principal was keen that I live on or near the college grounds so that I might "get to know the Africans" on a social basis – and have a place to which I could invite them. Regardless of whatever other motives he may have had, the prospect suited me well. And, on the face of it, the principal seemed to have created a rather special atmosphere. His was the only teacher-training school in Northern Rhodesia that had not gone out on strike the previous spring. His European staff were the only whites I met who did not refer to the Africans in a patronizing way. Mr B. seemed to have zeal and purpose that implied a belief in integration. But I felt my way with him cautiously, and he urged me not to make decisions in a hurry.

The next day Mr B. called at the hostel to talk further about possible living arrangements. "I seem to be only a burden to you so far," I told him.

"Well, I'll tell you honestly, when headquarters phoned up and asked did I want a woman from UNESCO I said, 'No, certainly not. I've got enough women around here.' What they should have done is send you to Chalimbana, where there are secondary teacher-training courses. They chose Kitwe probably because I'm an English specialist. I'm sure we'll work it out. They didn't tell me you were a woman of charm."

I laughed. More often, at home, I was told I came on too strong and men did not like that. "Charm won't be enough," I told him. "I can see that what you need is a science or arithmetic teacher here. Not an English teacher."

"We can use this term to fit you in, especially to help us tutor the girls. Some observation perhaps, although it's better if you start right in teaching as well." When he had covered all the matters on his mind he left, but not before I had told him that I could approve of Kitwe College because it seemed to stress race harmony. Mr B. nodded. He felt I would like the place, especially if I lived in it.

I found myself in the situation of having to buy a car from South African dealers. Mr N., who drove me about, demonstrating models, was a narrow-faced, narrow-eyed, dark, lean man with a pear-shaped head. He spoke English with a marked Boer accent and he often broke into Afrikaans. He had come to Lusaka because he would be paid better there than if he'd stayed in Joburg. His first remarks were all based on the white attitude of the times: Wherever I can do well financially, there I'll stay.

On my third visit, though I swear I had not given him a clue as to my attitudes, he sat in his office and launched into a diatribe. This was caused by the fact that he had telephoned a driving school for me, and the African who answered had failed to understand him. He explained that he wasn't interested in politics. Oh, no. The reason he had left South Africa was because he didn't like politics. "But there is one thing the world cannot understand, that an Afrikaner knows, and that is that these South African kaffirs are monkeys, not men. You can train a monkey to fetch and carry, but you can't train him to think. Just see what a mess they made of my command, 'Get the key.' No key is found. Ask for information, they hang up." He said all these things in a cold, hard, matter-of-fact voice, proselytizing nonetheless.

I felt amazingly calm, just saying I didn't agree. Anthropologists didn't agree either. Findings in Ghana, Nigeria and French Africa proved him wrong. He then recommenced on the same tack, about Africans and American Negroes being different, a higher type, but Rhodesians were monkeys.

I was a stranger in a strange state. I had expected this attitude; it was exactly as I would have defined it, but I was moved more to sorrow than to anger. And I felt that African resentment against these attitudes must have been such that it would be impossible for them to believe me, to accept me. Why should they?

At a village school, waiting for a bell to ring, a lesson to begin, I had a talk with Sky, the college chauffeur, as we sat in the Land Rover. We were in an African compound with ragged, barefoot children around us playing in the dust. A storm was brewing, seemingly ready to swoop down and break right over our heads; then it suddenly changed direction. Sky was at pains to tell me that his country, Nyasaland, was lovelier than this flat, dull countryside. "I lived by a lake with a mountain behind me," he said. If his land was so beautiful, I asked, why had he chosen to leave it? "There is no work for car drivers, chauffeurs," he explained. But nonetheless everything cost much less in Nyasaland.

I asked Sky what his wages were. "Fifteen pounds." Per week, I guessed. "No. By month." Although he got free housing, he had everything else to buy for his wife and three children – food, clothing, fuel. "In a day the money is gone," he said. How much would he get, I wondered aloud, if he worked at the mine? A chauffeur there, or a car mechanic, got about thirty pounds a month. A labourer, the same. A more skilled miner, an officer, would get over fifty pounds. I did not ask Sky how much a white miner would get.

After the brown beginnings of December I was happy to see how the rains were changing the soil to a dark, rich green. Shrubs with musk-scented flowers seemed to bound with vigorous life. Swallows and meadow birds swarmed from low bushes, singing. I noticed a strange sight: a huge tree, the left half abloom and leafy, the right with branches stripped, sere and autumnal. This was the mythical fig tree. Even in the flat countryside ancient reverberations emerged: colour for the eye, music for the ear.

Overhead, the sky stretched to the horizon, a misty blue, wide and elliptical like the sea. The dreamlike clouds, drifting without aim, could have reassembled at any moment and exploded in thunder. Reluctantly, I hastened back to my walled college enclosure.

The college day began well before 8:30 A.M. A bell called us to prayers in the hall, a multipurpose building. The principal was on the platform, framed by the staff. We faced the benches below, the rows of black faces and gleaming white shirts of the students, who stood and sat in an often rehearsed ritual. They did like to sing. I was not given to churchgoing, unless it was to a Quaker meeting, but I did enjoy the old evangelical hymns, especially Bunyan's "To Be a Pilgrim." Following the brief service, the principal rose to make the announcements. One of them concerned a Mrs. Macnair, from Canada, who was a poetry expert. The students laughed. I only got the significance of this later, when one of the African staff explained the bewilderment of the students. "You know the principal has a north-country accent. They thought he said you were a poultry expert." How I laughed. This was not an agricultural school, so why was this woman coming to tell them about chickens?

This matter was cleared up in due course when my students began to show curiosity and speak to me freely. "How strange for a widow to come alone to Africa instead of journeying to her brother–in–law's family." I explained that my brother–in–law lived in Scotland, and it did not seem sensible to travel there. I had to clear up this and other misconceptions.

That week David, as I had been invited to address the principal, sprang his first lesson on me. Instead of teaching his domestic science girls English, he marked their books at the back of the room, having given me a brief warning and a comprehension passage to read on "Initiations in Liberia." This led me to describe Canadian Indian customs first, then Liberian, then Rhodesian. My aim was to get the girls to talk about their own lives, their own customs. They did, with gusto. I felt it was the best lesson I had ever taught. Afterwards, David said not a word. But I did learn the next day that he was planning a program for me that would be all English teaching and tutoring. I was delighted. I was to go into the African compounds and schoolrooms to watch African teacher trainees teach at the primary level.

Evenings in Kitwe could be quite educational for the newcomer. At the domestic science girls' party, the great Dorothy Livesay was a bit shaken to find herself playing a game in which each person on a relay team had to pick up a lemon that was nestling under another girl's chin, then, without hands touching it, tuck it under her own chin and run to the other end of the line. This involved close physical contact with the girl in front of you and the girl behind. I did not recoil from the contact, but it was hot and different, a totally new experience.

Another relationship I was having to deal with was that of the whites and the blacks in a community situation. For instance: During the coffee break, staff gathered in the common room with all the white teachers on one side and all the black on the other. I walked from the coffee table right over to the black side.

"They are so extravagant with water," exclaimed a white wife on inspection duty of the humble three-room brick houses. "And water costs so much here." I wondered how many baths her family had per day, with hot water; married students had only an outdoor cold tap for washing and drinking. And how much she spent on food for her family. The school was allowed twenty-two pounds per year for feeding each single student; this included bedding, equipment replacement and cleaning materials. The diet consisted mainly of mealy meal, two pounds of vegetables and two-and-a-half pounds of meat per week. Extras would be small portions of milk, rice, sugar and bread – on weekends.

Some days flowed very well, others seemed blocked by insuperables. One day, Miss M. and Peter asked me for advice on their teaching methods. My feeling was that more oral work and particularly some play-reading and acting out would help liven the interest in English.

I had a long talk with Felix C., the African teacher of handwriting. He only had Standard Four, six years schooling, but he was teaching teachers. He was quite beautiful – his face had that Egyptian look often seen in Northern Rhodesia. After talking about his education and his doubts whether it was worth continuing, now that he had married, he told me of his real interests: carving, sculpting and painting. He had wanted to go to art school, and this had been promised to him if he could complete Standard Four. Then he had been told he must complete Standard Six at least. He did not see any point in this. At school, Felix had had a botany teacher who encouraged his drawing. He began to carve and model, too, after studying his own face in the mirror. Soon he was able to sell his clay torsos. Then another teacher taught him how to paint with oils, but he felt he needed to know more, more.

I had hoped I would gain more scope when the principal assigned me to library work. Up till then different teachers had led their students to the locked and barred cupboards, the shelves three-quarters empty. The assortment contained many of that type of "classic" and abridged book that one relegated to the attic. The former librarian, Miss C., went through them with me and then we went shopping at the local bookstore in Kitwe. David had given her only fifty pounds after promising her one hundred. Once we had some up-to-date books, we faced the problem of how to get the students to respect them, when everyone expected them to be stolen. I suggested having open shelves. "You could try," Miss C. replied doubtfully. I thought for a moment and said, "We'll make a co-op out of it. The students will be in charge."

Full of enthusiasm, I went to the Kitwe Public Library to inquire about taking some selected students there to be shown how the indexing system worked.

"You mean you would be bringing Africans?" the girl at the desk asked.

"Certainly."

"Oh-h. I don't think that would be possible."

"Do you mean to say that the public library of Kitwe won't lend books to Africans?"

"But this isn't a public library. You have to pay for membership."

"I see," I said. And, yes, I saw. I might in my dudgeon have stomped out then and there, but I pursued the topic, asking if they might admit a group of students – not as members, but as observers.

"Oh, that would be all right, I should think. Yes. There would be someone here who could explain how we function, but you had best come in the morning, early. There are too many people here in the afternoons."

That week I had a fascinating evening, accompanying G., the government adult education officer, to several night schools. He introduced me to some seven or eight classes, before which I was asked to speak on UNESCO and answer questions. These young Africans worked all day, cycled home for dinner, often as much as three miles, and then back to a two-hour night class – five nights a week. Their keenness and enthusiasm were most encouraging to see. They were thirsting for knowledge of the world outside and how they could find help. In more mature classes, sixth-form work, questions were fired at me. In the whole evening, I saw six women. But there *were* six. I found myself giving a different kind of pep talk in each class, introducing a different slant on UNESCO.

G. was the finest young European I had met there, the most liberal-minded and enthusiastic. It was his house I was going to move into when he went on leave at Christmas: a lovely thatched-roof, African-type house, set among banana, mango, papaw and bamboo trees. It was roomy, airy and cool. I had no equipment to buy and I inherited his houseboy, Wilson. By the time the new term opened in mid-January I was settled into my happiest months in Northern Rhodesia.

After the spring term of teacher training at Kitwe, I could look back to see what cooperation with the students had accomplished. They were in charge of the library service, with new books purchased (some through UNESCO). For the first time, I believe, they had put on one of Shakespeare's plays – *The Merchant of Venice*. Of course they performed it their way, full speed ahead. "What did that matter?" I asked the English staff, who were not complimentary. My students, however, loved acting out the roles, especially those of Shylock and

Portia. More significant for me was my growing friendship with Ralph, who translated some of the text into Bemba for the enthusiastic audience, and who was my right-hand man in all doubtful situations. For instance, he explained to me why the male actors refused to wear tunics in the Elizabethan style: their knees had to be covered. Thus I learned about male modesty.

But more importantly, I was into a deep psychic relationship with Raphael, whom we all called Ralph. He was a young married man whose wife and child lived in a village far away, as was custom among most students. Ralph, very black, but with a somewhat European visage and carriage, had been through a Catholic mission school and was determined to write the O level Cambridge examinations. Naturally, I gave him extra coaching, and as if in return he arranged that I drive us to be part of a village wedding ceremony. I heard an old uncle haranguing the bridegroom, as he laid a bare knife on the gift table. In the tent I saw and heard the drums and the circle of dancing led by the mother-in-law.

From time to time, Ralph also explained to me the political situation in the Rhodesias involving the UNIP (United Independent Party) program for one man, one vote and "Kwatcha," freedom. A longish poem of mine, "The Second Language," celebrates this dialectic. From this I quote the section "Politics":

On the village green
circled by huts
shaded by palm trees
a woman was speaking:
tall, gaunt, with flexing arms
she swayed like a dance
from one side of the crowd to the other
shouting in Bemba
the language cleaving and cutting the air
as her arms flayed.

A fluttering crowd of women
in kerchiefs and coloured shawls
baby weighted, shifted
listened:
men lolled on the sidelines
black trousers, white shirts.
They showed their teeth, mocking
or shouting approval.

What does she say? I asked you:
You listened, frowning.
She says, if the men are cowards
they fear authority
they tremble in the face of the police
she says:
If the men will not act
the women will!
the women are fearless.

And is she right, Raphael
is she right?

I do not know, you said
I do not go with violence
nor violent women.

It is easy to kill
you said —
and led me away quickly.

When living and teaching at Kitwe I sometimes had occasion to go
to conferences led by British experts in the teaching of English as a
second language. One of these was held in Ndola, which is south of

D.L. with Ralph, her friend and colleague, at Kitwe, 1962

Lusaka and on the way to Salisbury, Southern Rhodesia (now Zimbabwe). There I had the good fortune to find another new friend, Prisca Molotsi. She taught geography at a women's college in Lusaka and was one of those married women who were ablaze with the desire to improve the lot of women and children. In spite of protocol, I stayed with her family and she returned the visit to stay with me at Kitwe. We have been close friends ever since.

Prisca has since been a delegate to world feminist conferences. In 1986, she got a grant to take university courses in Los Angeles; that summer she visited me on Galiano Island. We've managed to communicate at least once a year. "Freedom" under Kaunda has indeed changed women's lot in 1991; Prisca has written, "You would not dream, Dee, how much things have changed for women's development." Yes, I would love to see it. But I know how difficult life must still be for Zambians – without access to the sea or to the South African railway the economy cannot really flourish.

Chalimbana was a different kettle of fish. By the end of the school year at Kitwe, I had made arrangements with UNESCO headquarters in Paris and the educational officer in Lusaka to continue my appointment by moving to Chalimbana Training College near Lusaka. It was a college for higher-level teachers and would be more suited to explaining methods of teaching English for secondary-school pupils. I felt that I had more to give mature student teachers who were already conversant in English.

They were a very eager class of about twenty men and ten women. I soon found that I had the same curriculum problem: how to teach for examinations when they were tied to a totally different culture. All the textbooks were geared to Cambridge O levels. So, for example, how to teach Wordsworth? On a Saturday I drove my Volkswagen to Lusaka and found, in a hat shop, a wreath of ornamental daffodils. These I tossed about the classroom as we ventured into

I wandered lonely as a cloud
That floats on high o'er vales and hills,
When all at once I saw a crowd,
A host, of golden daffodils ...

The keenest students, however, like Howard Silanda, the head of the class, were more excited when I gave them Margaret Laurence's first novel, *This Side Jordan*. That a white woman, a Canadian, could come so near to the truth about Africans astonished and pleased them. They were much less enthused by D. H. Lawrence's *The Plumed Serpent*, recommended by Mr. George, head of English curriculum. They were moved instead by the harrowing tale of George Eliot's *Mill on the Floss*.

When I think now about Chalimbana I remember the faces: Howard, so sturdy and reliable on campus, but very carefree when we drove with his family along the northern route to the Congo. He pleaded that I let him practise driving. His wife, Doreen, and babe were in the back seat, and as we drove faster and faster she called out faintly until I seized the ignition key and we swayed to a stop. Nothing was said; I took over the wheel.

Later, Howard was very helpful in explaining what I did right and what I did wrongly in my role as women's warden. I had argued with the English principal, an Anglican priest, that I had not come to Northern Rhodesia to be a women's warden. It would be much better if that role were filled by an African woman who understood how to handle the girls. It turned out, however, that not only was I to be women's warden, I also had to teach the secondary-school boys first-year French. My main job of course was teaching literature and grammar to the older students, men and women. They were delighted when I brought in taped exercises on pronunciation. One morning we practised for an hour so loudly that Mr. George next door protested vehemently to the principal. A happier situation was directing the cast for an outdoor production of *Androcles and the Lion*. The girls had great fun designing the costumes, especially making a lion's head. One of them, a very pretty girl named Rose Ichanga, was often at my house talking about her hopes. I discovered she was doing some delightful watercolour paintings of local village scenes. Indeed, she gave me one, which I have framed, called "Women at the Riverside." But for the most part, the women in my class had little hope of developing their talents or even learning any skills so that they could become office workers or nurses.

Ironically, I began to have the feeling that working with these mature students was doing my understanding more good than anything I could give them. Just the way they lived their music was fascinating for me. In their dining hut, for example, dancing began before breakfast and sometimes I joined in, erasing all my inhibitions about being able to fit in with a partner. No one needed a partner. We were all partners, linked to the drums and the handmade instruments. On one memorable evening, three or four of them came to my house, bringing their instruments for me to put on tape. I also taped a number of the women's singing dances. For me, life had become part of the music.

I should not leave my description of Chalimbana without mentioning two more fine members of the staff. One was Dai Davies, the Welshman in charge of construction and upkeep. He reminded me vividly of my friend in New Jersey, Scotty, because he was broad and stocky. Dai had a warmth for and an enjoyment of people, whatever their colour and background. I don't know how he came to be in Africa, leaving his wife in England, but he loved to tell of his years as a stage carpenter in the British film industry. At Chalimbana he became very friendly with an American couple who lived in close harmony with the Bantu people. George Corinaldi was a man of colour who taught social studies. His beautiful wife, originally from France, had never quite identified with this foreign country. I had the feeling she longed for the break which would come around for staff on furlough. George, however, became completely integrated with his Bantu students and their point of view. None of us whites could have the same rapport. George, now a widower, has been teaching in the U.S. and has kept in touch with Dai throughout these thirty years. Dai in turn has sent yearly Christmas greetings to all of us who were on the staff and has visited Canada several times.

During the Christmas holidays of 1961, my daughter, Marcia, and I were reunited in the south of France. My Provençal friend Agnès was now living in Toulon with her husband and daughter. So we had a great celebration of friendship. My stay there, however, was suddenly cut short, as I described in this letter to Alan Crawley:

January 2, 1962
Chalimbana
My Dear Alan:

I enjoyed having your Christmas news when I got home here, rather unexpectedly. The French Africa Line had neglected to notify Salisbury that my booked return trip, January 2, had been scratched. There's only one plane a week, so I had to make a decision in ten minutes and get ready to leave Toulon for Nice, by train, in four hours' time. It was a difficult shock to give Marcy, serenely waiting for me by the seashore. However, I was sure she could cope, and carry out plans for stopping off in Paris after New Year's, going the rounds of galleries with Dorothy Willis. As it turned out, she missed this frightful winter spell in London and Ireland. In Toulon though, we had mainly wet or grey weather and were both chilled, there being no central heating. Had to buy woolly underwear, wool stockings, rubber boots, etc. — at outrageous French prices. And then, the day after I left, it soared to seventy! So I could have used my bathing suit!

For me, it was rather good to get down to sea level and also to feel cold again. I slept all night through, and I stopped being hungry and thirsty all the time (as here). Lost a pound or two, I think; so have passed a New Year's resolution not to drink any more beer (so Peter will recognize me in June). Also, it is a strange experience taking on an old self; I immediately became introspective, observant, sensitive to sights and sounds and characters; and wrote a poem the first day! I shall hope one day in the next seven years to settle in Aix for a time, and write.

It is as natural as breathing once I'm there.

After one week, though, I began to dream of Africa; and my waking thoughts turned that way all the time. I felt Marcy was accepting me too easily and nestling under the wing; so when I suddenly had to go, I was emotionally ready. Perhaps it was a shock for her; but it is through these shocks, I expect, that we get launched and onto our own feet.

Now I am happily here; mostly alone, as all the students are away. It is quite serene, the soft landscape yielding to rain. I can call on people (staff) if I want to, but don't really want to, as yet. Have grown to like my own company! And I do have a lot of English reading to do, before the term starts on the 5th.

So many thanks for the promised sending of journals. Marcy and I were astounded to see, in a Belfast paper, that there really was a Katanga developing in Quebec. We thought you were only joking! I can't find any reference to it anywhere else.

The secondary boys will love the stickers.

As I love you. Stick that onto your ribs!

On March 4, 1962, I received a warning that I was being watched by the police.

The weather had turned. The rains seemed far away on the horizon, resting in soft clouds. A wind blew; the sun stayed warm, glowing not burning. All was still green, green; the waving elephant grass was nearly as high as a person. Birds and butterflies were at their happiest, because it was still moist on the ground. The river was running. I saw a new bird on that day's walk – just a swooping flash of dark, with a long, long black tail – a swallow with a kite attached. The lantana, declared a noxious weed, burned with its orange suns on every wild hedge.

So I walked around the hill with my dog, Cappy, past the Women's School building, through the "marrieds" village, where little girls wore too-long dresses and little black boys ran naked. A skinny brown pup rushed out and yapped at Cappy (the table turned) and women gathering in their yards, braiding each other's hair, laughed to see Cappy run. They smiled good afternoon. Around to the brow of the hill and down, down into the valley through the agricultural station: radios playing in every thatched house, families sitting together under trees.

Along the main driveway a man, resting on his lawn as he talked with a friend, hailed me and he came up to the roadside to chat. He reminded me that I had given him a lift to a United Independence Party meeting. I remembered. So, he had had a time, because the policeman there – I think he meant a European (not one of the African police) – told him he had no business to be bringing a European woman near the place. They did not want any white people at those meetings. What was she doing anyway, the policeman wanted to know. The man replied he thought I had been bringing my houseboy to the meeting.

"No," I corrected him. "We were just going to Mpansha's store for wood, but we wanted to see what the meeting was like. It was raining, though. No one seemed to be there. Did anyone come later?"

"No," he said. "Not many. It wasn't a big meeting. A hundred came. But the police, he kept asking about you. I said you were a teacher."

"So you think the police are watching me?"

"Well, I wanted to tell you. It is known – the students tell it – you are interested. And these are the times when everything is turned around."

"Things are upside-down," I agreed.

"So then some time after, this police he came to my house. We had a long talk – two hours – all politics. He said he could not want to be under an African. He is superior, see? And he asked me again about the European lady. I said, 'I do not know about her. She is a teacher. Maybe she is from Lusaka.' "

I thanked him. I think he was genuine. He had not sought me out to warn me, but as soon as he saw me he came to report, quite forthrightly.

I went home the back way, by the tennis court, and met a young man of eight or nine carrying a Catholic prayer book. "Good afternoon, madame." "Good afternoon – sir," said I. Did he notice, I wonder? Anyway, he came running after me, asking in very good

English if I had the picture I had taken of him and his little sister. "In your doorway? Down near the Women's School?"

"Yes, please."

So I brought him to the house and showed him the colour slide; then I found he was Samuel Inglese, the handicraft teacher's son, and that he was in Form 3A, where I often sat watching students teach. "I am in 3A, but I can read," he assured me. "Have you any book for me to read?" I found a book of fables and he proved he could tackle it by reading aloud. I lent him the book and gave him the photo. "If I bring the baby to your garden will you take a more nice one? Not at our house. In front of your flowers?"

I looked at the sky. It had begun to cloud a little. "When the sun shines," I said. "Come again with the baby."

He ran off, hugging the photo and book to his heart.

Like the Japanese riddle of the man who dreamed he was a butterfly: was he a human or was he the butterfly dreaming he was a human? Am I that Canadian lady? Or am I a young black boy hugging his baby sister, asking to be frozen in a photograph?

In the summer of 1963 I returned to Canada, to Vancouver, to settle down with my children, who would be attending classes at UBC. From my UNESCO savings I was able to buy a house in Kitsilano, close to the university, where I could teach creative writing courses. My passionate interest in Zambia sought and found release in mingling with young poets of the TISH group, who likewise were stimulated by other poets – the Black Mountain crowd. What a summer that was, mingling with Earle Birney's selection of poetry-makers. I became so keen on the new movement that I applied to do an M.Ed. on the subject: "Rhythm and Sound in Contemporary Canadian Poetry." That thesis was accepted in 1965. More important, at that time many of my poems from *The Unquiet Bed* and *Plainsongs* were written, poems that freely expressed the pent-up passion within me. Its origin had been the Zambian experience.

After Words

At the outset of these journeyings, I mentioned some of the hurdles that might lie ahead, in the search for "the truth." I was to learn that some doors are locked and will not open. Recently I have been offered an illumination by a long-time friend from university days. Ross Parmenter, a journalist and researcher, suggests that the differences between biography and autobiography are wide. The biographer seeks to delve into every nook and cranny, whereas the autobiographer selects what she/he feels to be the most significant events, happenings, traumas.

In this book I have not dwelt on problems relating to being a woman, such as how to earn a living in a man's world; widowhood; alcoholism; aging, or health. To write an account of my role as mother of two and grandmother of seven would be a larger task than is contemplated here, although remembering all those childhoods is one of the great pleasures of growing old. I have been at pains to deal with many of the events that determined my development as a teacher, a social worker, a humanist and a poet. Beyond 1963, my return from Zambia, many other lives have crisscrossed with mine. Since these people are living, and still vulnerable, I have chosen not to write about them here.

Books by
Dorothy Livesay

Green Pitcher. Toronto: Macmillan of Canada, 1928.

Signpost. Toronto: Macmillan of Canada, 1932.

Day and Night. Toronto: Ryerson; Boston: Bruce Humphries, 1944.

Poems for People. Toronto: Ryerson, 1947.

Call My People Home. Toronto: Ryerson, 1950.

New Poems. Toronto: Emblem Books, 1955.

Selected Poems, 1926-1956. Toronto: Ryerson, 1957.

The Colour of God's Face. Vancouver: Unitarian Service Committee, 1964.

The Unquiet Bed (illustrated by Roy Kiyooka). Toronto: Ryerson, 1967.

The Documentaries: Selected Longer Poems. Toronto: Ryerson, 1968.

Plainsongs. Fredericton, N.B.: Fiddlehead Poetry Books, 1969.

Disasters of the Sun. Burnaby, B.C.: Blackfish, 1971.

Collected Poems: The Two Seasons. Toronto and New York: McGraw-Hill Ryerson, 1972.

Nine Poems of Farewell, 1972-1973. Windsor, Ontario: Black Moss, 1973.

A Winnipeg Childhood. Winnipeg: Peguis, 1973. Reprinted under the title *Beginnings: A Winnipeg Childhood.* Toronto: New Press, 1975. Revised edition published under the title *Beginnings.* Winnipeg: Peguis, 1988.

Ice Age. Erin, Ontario: Press Porcepic, 1975.

The Woman I Am. Erin, Ontario: Press Porcepic, 1977. Revised edition. Montreal: Guernica, 1991.

Right Hand Left Hand: A True Life of the Thirties, edited by David Arnason and Kim Todd. Erin, Ontario: Press Porcepic, 1977.

The Raw Edges: Voices from Our Time. Winnipeg: Turnstone, 1981.

The Phases of Love. Toronto: Coach House, 1983.

Feeling the Worlds: New Poems. Fredericton, N.B.: Goose Lane Editions, 1984.

The Self-Completing Tree: Selected Poems. Victoria: Press Porcepic, 1986.

Les Âges de l'amour. Translated by Jean Antonin Billard. (Originally published as *The Phases of Love*.) Montreal: Guernica, 1989.

The Husband. Charlottetown, P.E.I.: Ragweed, 1990.

Dorothy Livesay's papers are housed in the Department of Archives and Special Collections, 331, Elizabeth Dafoe Library (3rd floor), University of Manitoba, Winnipeg, Manitoba R3T 2N2 (204-474-9986).